E COLL... ...TION

BFARSDEN

r... ...efore th...

Autistic Children

LORNA WING MD DPM

Autistic Children

A GUIDE FOR PARENTS

CONSTABLE LONDON

First published in 1971
by Constable & Co Ltd
10 Orange Street London WC2H 7EG
Copyright © 1971 by Lorna Wing
Reprinted 1972
Revised edition 1975
ISBN 0 09 458390 0

Printed in Great Britain by
REDWOOD BURN LIMITED
Trowbridge & Esher

Preface

Autistic children were first described as a special group by Professor Leo Kanner in the early 1940's. Now, in 1971, the underlying causes of early childhood autism are still unknown, and the possibility of their discovery seems as far away as ever. On the other hand, much progress has been made in understanding the handicaps of children who are already affected, and in ways of helping them to learn social and practical skills.

In writing this present book, I have drawn on the work of doctors, psychologists and teachers with long experience in the field; but I could not have written the book at all without the help of the many parents who have, through patience and determination, found ways of coping with the never-ending series of problems presented by living with an autistic child.

L.W.

Contents

Part I
Description of the children

I

Introduction

The mental and physical development of children can go wrong in many different ways, and sometimes this leads to difficult behaviour. Autism is one of the ways in which disturbed development may be shown. Autistic children appear at first sight to be strikingly different from normal children, and from children with the commoner kinds of childhood disabilities. However, each of the problems they show can be found in other handicapped children, especially in those with some rather rare congenital defects affecting perception and language development. It is easier for parents to deal with the situation if they can see their child as handicapped, sharing problems with other handicapped children, but also remembering that he is first and foremost a child, with the same need as every other child for a home and family, love, security, guidance and a chance to develop his skills and positive assets to the full. Each autistic child has his own personality which determines the way he reacts to his handicaps and which makes him a unique individual. For these reasons, parents and others who work with these children do not like to hear them referred to as 'autistics', which suggests that the handicap is the only thing that matters. They are children who happen to be suffering from the condition known as early childhood autism.

DEFINITIONS

One of the biggest problems in writing about autistic

children is that doctors and other professional people tend
to differ in the words they use to describe and name the
condition. The cause, or causes, of autism in children are,
as yet, unknown, and there are no neat tests which can be
used to make the diagnosis. Blood tests, X-rays, electro-
encephalograms (that is, records of the electrical waves
from the brain), and other physical examinations which are
helpful in general medicine, cannot give a positive answer
to the question 'Is this child autistic?', although they are
sometimes necessary to detect or exclude other conditions
which might be present. The only way to make a positive
diagnosis is for the doctor to ask about the child's behaviour,
in minute detail, from birth up to the time of examination,
because the decision depends upon the presence or absence
of a special pattern of behaviour.

In this situation, people look for theories to explain the
children's odd behaviour, and the different names that are
used are linked with some of the ideas that have been put
forward. Professor Kanner suggested the name 'early
infantile autism' because he believed that the aloofness and
social withdrawal shown in the early years were the most
important features. ('Autism', used in psychiatry to mean
withdrawn and self-absorbed, comes from the Greek word
'autos', meaning 'self'.) Other workers refer to the condition as 'childhood schizophrenia', because they believe that
it is a special form of the adult illness.* Others again have
used very general terms, such as 'childhood psychosis',

---

* This theory is being discarded nowadays, for several reasons.
Firstly, the symptoms of autism are different from those of schizophrenia. For example, delusions and hallucinations are important in
the latter and never seen in the former, and the speech problems of
autism are not at all the same as those found in some schizophrenic
patients. Secondly, when autistic children grow up, they do not become
schizophrenic adults. Thirdly, schizophrenic patients are more likely
than average to have relatives who are also schizophrenic. Autistic
children, on the other hand, have only the same chance of having a

'severe emotional disturbance', 'non-communicating children' or 'exceptional children', but these labels can cover so many different behaviour patterns that they cause more problems than they solve.

In this book I shall try to avoid confusion over names by defining terms in simple concrete ways, and in some detail. There are many different ideas as to what a 'psychosis' is, but I shall use the label 'childhood psychosis' to cover all those conditions in which a child behaves most or all of the time in ways which are extremely strange and unpredictable, even considering his age and his level of intelligence. Many children who are backward act in a way which is strange for their physical age, but which is understandable if you know that they are mentally retarded. They are therefore not called psychotic. On the other hand, some children have patterns of behaviour which are unusual whatever their level of mental development and when this odd behaviour is continuous the children can be said to be psychotic. The term is a description and not an explanation of behaviour. Sometimes the cause of a childhood psychosis is known. It may be, for example, a brain tumour, some brain injury, or an infection in early childhood. More often, however, it is not possible to find any definite reason for the behaviour because, as yet, methods of examining the function of the brain are limited.

The term 'childhood psychosis' covers many different patterns of behaviour of which early childhood autism is one, and perhaps the commonest, example. The behaviour shown by autistic children will be described in detail in Chapter 4 below.

---

schizophrenic relative as the average (and some say the chance is less than average). The only similarity is that both schizophrenic adults and autistic children are very vulnerable to the effects of bad institutions, but this goes for other kinds of illnesses too.

History

It seems likely that there have always been autistic children, although it is only in the last twenty-five years that they have been named as a group and thought of separately from other severely mentally handicapped children. Perhaps they were the reason for the legends of 'fairy changeling' children, in which the fairies were believed to steal away a human baby and leave a fairy child in its place. In some versions of the story the changeling was remarkably beautiful, but strange and remote from human kind.

In 1799 a French doctor, J. M. G. Itard, was given charge of a boy about twelve years old, known as Victor the 'Wild boy of Aveyron', who had been found wandering and living wild in the woods. The child's behaviour was very abnormal. Itard thought that he was handicapped because he had been isolated from humans from an early age. Pinel, another eminent doctor of the time, disagreed with Itard over this, and believed that the boy was severely mentally retarded from birth. Reading the story now, it is possible to see that Victor behaved like an autistic child. Some people have suggested that he was autistic because he was abandoned in infancy. It seems much more likely that he was separated from, or abandoned by, his parents in the troubled times following the French Revolution *because* he was autistic and difficult to manage, and not the other way round. Itard's story is most interesting and moving, and worth reading because of the way in which he set about teaching the boy.

Over a century later, in 1919, an American psychologist,

Lightner Witmer, wrote an article about Don, a boy of two years and seven months, who also behaved like an autistic child, and who was accepted at Witmer's special school. Individual teaching over a long period helped this child to compensate for his handicaps.

Professor Kanner, in 1943, was the first person to describe these children as a special group. Since then interest has grown steadily. Many different theories of causes have been put forward, and the actual behaviour of the children has been studied in more detail. Within the last ten years parents' societies have grown up in many countries and they have worked for earlier diagnosis, better services and especially for more and better opportunities for special education for the children. However, there is still a long way to go, even in those countries where there is provision for special education for handicapped children.

How many children are autistic?

This question was answered by a special study done in the English county of Middlesex in 1964. Every child with a home address in the county who was aged eight, nine or ten was considered in this study, whether or not he had any known mental or physical handicap. It seems that, in this age group at any rate, between four and five children in every 10,000 will have autistic behaviour. Another study in Denmark gave the same result. The chances are that this number of autistic children will be found in any industrialised country. In areas where many children die young, the numbers may be smaller, since autistic babies and toddlers are sometimes difficult to rear because of feeding problems.

Autistic behaviour almost always begins from birth or within the first two and a half (rarely three) years of life. Children can become psychotic at any time in childhood, but if the change occurs after infancy or early childhood the pattern of behaviour is not the same as in autism. Professor Kanner at first thought that autism always began from birth (hence the name early *infantile* autism), but later he described some children who developed autistic behaviour after a period of apparently normal development. For this reason, I shall use the name early *childhood* autism in this book.

Boys are affected more often than girls. Some people have found four times as many boys, but in the Middlesex study it was a little less than three boys to one girl. Many autistic children are the first-born in their families, but it is difficult to know if this has any real significance.

There is some evidence that autistic children are more likely to have had complications around the time of their birth than their normal brothers and sisters.* Approximately one-third of all autistic children have some other handicap affecting their brain or central nervous system, such as spasticity, epilepsy, hydrocephalus, or a history of meningitis or encephalitis (inflammation of the brain). The others seem to be physically normal, although careful examination does show various special problems (see Chapter 4).

Kanner thought that children with other handicaps should not be put into the same group as the children with 'early infantile autism', but in some cases children with extra handicaps behave in exactly the same way as the children described by Kanner, so there seems no good reason not to include them. In any case, some of the children diagnosed as typically autistic develop symptoms of other handicaps, such as epilepsy, later on in childhood or adolescence.

Children who show early childhood autism in its most classic form are likely to have parents who are of higher intelligence and educational level than average. Professor Kanner first pointed this out, but some workers argued that this was a false impression. They thought it was due to the fact that better-educated people might refuse to believe that their child was severely retarded and would have the knowledge (and money) to go to specialists who knew about autism. However, the results of the Middlesex study show that Kanner had good reasons for his view. In this study all the children with autistic behaviour in the chosen age group were examined, whether or not their parents had taken them to specialists. It was found that the parents of the most typically autistic children (mothers as well as fathers) were as a group more intelligent and

*But this appears to be true only of those with the more severe handicaps.

better educated than the average for Middlesex, although there were individual exceptions.

To sum up, autism is a condition beginning in infancy or early childhood. It occurs about as often as total deafness in childhood and more often than total blindness. It is common enough to make it likely that most people will meet at least one autistic child at some time or another in their lives.

The behaviour of autistic children

Each autistic child is an individual, and is different in many ways from other children with the same diagnosis. This is partly because the condition may be present in any degree varying from very mild to very severe, but also because each child has his own personality which somehow comes through despite his handicaps. Any description has to be a generalisation, and very few children have all the symptoms that I shall describe. Most of them change as they grow older, since the problems may become less marked, and some disappear altogether. Nevertheless, the children do have a special type of behaviour pattern in common, especially in the earlier years of childhood.

BABYHOOD

Some babies who will become autistic children appear to develop normally for a time, and their parents do not notice anything unusual in the first year or two (although careful questioning may show that these children, as babies, showed little active interest in their surroundings). Other babies give their parents cause for concern almost from birth. Sometimes mothers say that they felt something was wrong within the first few days, but they usually cannot tell why they had this feeling. Feeding problems are fairly common, and some of the babies do not suck well.

There seem to be two kinds of autistic babies, among those who are obviously abnormal from birth. Some scream a great deal during both day and night, especially on waking from sleep, and cannot be comforted or soothed. The only way to stop the crying may be a ride in a pram or a car and the screaming usually starts again when the motion ceases. The baby may be stiff and hard to cuddle, and may fight against everything, including being washed, dressed and changed.

The second kind of autistic baby is placid and undemanding, content to lie quietly in his pram all day. Sometimes mothers feel that a child of this kind does not know when he is hungry because he never cries for food and would starve unless fed as a routine. This type of child is less exhausting than the first, and less obviously worrying, but parents become concerned as time goes on and the child does not become more active.

One of the things most often noticed by mothers is that their autistic baby never lifts up his arms or makes himself ready to be picked up. When lifted up the children do not snuggle down comfortably in their mother's arms, and later on do not grip with their hands and knees if carried pick-a-back.

Some autistic babies lie in their prams and scratch or tap on the cover for long periods of time, and some rock or bang their heads when left alone. They may be fascinated by lights, or by anything that shines and twinkles. On the other hand they seem uninterested in the things which catch the attention of a normal baby as he grows and develops. Autistic babies do not lean out of their prams in eager curiosity to look at people and animals and the passing traffic, nor do they try to attract their mother's attention to these things by pointing and making excited noises.

This lack of interest makes parents wonder if their child is severely mentally retarded, but they usually do not accept this possibility because autistic babies tend to smile, cut their teeth, sit up, crawl and walk at the usual ages, and gain weight normally, once early feeding problems have passed. Sometimes the milestones are later than normal, but this is more likely in a child who has other handicaps as well as autism. However, mothers may say that their baby smiled when tickled, cuddled or bounced up and down, but not when looking at someone's face. They may also remember that he did not bother to sit up even when he was able to, apparently because the world was of little interest to him. A number of the children stand up and walk round the furniture at the right time, but may be reluctant to let go and walk without support until many months after the usual age.

TWO TO FIVE YEARS OF AGE

This is the stage when autistic behaviour is most obvious. If a child has been autistic from birth, it may be a long time before his parents put their fears and suspicions into words, but they usually become seriously worried by the time he is two or three years old, when he is most difficult to manage. If, on the other hand, the child has appeared normal from birth but has a marked change of behaviour occurring over a few weeks, his parents are likely to be alerted much more quickly to the gravity of the problem.

Young autistic children, especially those who have no other handicaps which might affect their appearance, seem to be physically healthy and are often unusually attractive. They have large eyes which do not look directly at other people. They seem to be aloof and unaffected by the world, interested only in some special object such as a smooth pebble or an empty box. If this object is lost, or if a familiar routine is disturbed, then the quiet remote child becomes a bundle of fury until his temper tantrum expires as quickly as it started – as if a tap had been turned off.

These 'typical' symptoms are so striking in early childhood that they tend to attract all the attention. This is a pity because this odd behaviour follows from other, more fundamental, handicaps, and it is impossible to understand and help an autistic child unless you know about the underlying problems which make it so hard for him to understand the world. The best way to describe them is to take each area of difficulty in turn and give some examples actually observed in autistic children. For the sake of simplicity I shall concentrate upon the kind of child who was autistic from birth or early babyhood.

PROBLEMS IN UNDERSTANDING THE WORLD

i *Unusual responses to sounds*

People often think that an autistic child is deaf because he tends to ignore very loud sounds, and not even blink if someone drops a pile of plates behind him. His parents usually know that he can hear because they notice that he turns round at once if, for example, a sweet is unwrapped behind him (that is, if he likes the kinds of sweets that are wrapped in paper). In 1799 Itard wrote about Victor: 'Of all his senses the ear appeared least sensitive. It was found, nevertheless that the sound of a cracking walnut or other favourite eatable never failed to make him turn round . . . yet this same organ showed itself insensible to the loudest of noises and the explosion of firearms.'

A child may be fascinated by some sounds such as that made by friction-drive toys or the ringing of a bell. Yet again he may find some sounds intensely distressing and will cover his ears and cringe away from the roar of a motor bike or the barking of a dog (though the children never seem to be sensitive to their own screams and shouts). These different responses may be seen in the same child within a short space of time.

ii *Difficulties in understanding speech*

A young autistic child's response to speech is just as

unusual as the way he reacts to other sounds. Around one year of age, when a normal child loves to hear his mother speak to him and shows his delight with his whole body, the autistic child pays no more attention to speech than to any other noise. On the whole he ignores it, although a loud shout may make him distressed, or he may be fascinated by a gentle whisper. He seems unaware that speech has a meaning, although he may attend if he hears one of the few words he knows that are linked with things he likes ('sweet', 'dinner', 'orange drink'). It may be some years before he learns to come when his own name is called. At this stage he does not obey any verbal instructions, listen to any warnings, or comprehend if he is scolded. It is easy to see that bringing up an autistic child presents many problems.

Later on, usually near the age of five, many autistic children begin to acquire some limited comprehension of speech. They will obey simple instructions such as 'Put on your coat' or 'Come to dinner'. Later still they may be able to understand enough to 'Give this to Daddy', as long as Father is in the same room. Any complication (such as too many instructions in the same sentence) will confuse the child, so that he becomes angry or upset or else withdraws and does nothing. An older child who likes to help may do the wrong thing in response to a complex sentence. One little girl was asked to 'Bring Mummy your jumper which is on the chair in your bedroom'. The child trotted upstairs and after several minutes staggered in with the chair.

iii *Difficulties when talking*

Some autistic children never speak, but remain mute all their lives. Others (probably slightly more than half) do learn to say at least a few words, although they almost always begin much later than normal. They usually start by repeating words spoken by other people, especially the last word or the last few words of a sentence. Often the exact accent of the speaker may be copied, and the pitch of his voice. The repetition of words seems to have little meaning for the child, and this empty echoing (like a parrot) is called 'echolalia'. Some children repeat words or phrases they have heard in the past and this is called 'delayed echolalia'. It occasionally happens that a child will produce one of these echoed phrases at an appropriate moment. For example, he might have a habit of saying 'You've left the door open' over and over again. Occasionally this will fit the situation and it will appear that the child knows what he is saying. It is easy to be misled into thinking that the child understands more than he really does, unless you know him well and realise that he repeats the things other people have said whether or not they are appropriate.

Some children never pass this stage, but others move on to the next, when they begin to say some words and phrases they work out for themselves, and which do have meaning. At first a child will name things that he wants, such as 'sweetie', 'drink', 'ice-cream'. He may then, after months or years, go on to use phrases. It is easy to tell the difference between a phrase that the child is echoing because he has heard it used by someone else and a phrase he has made up himself. The first comes out quickly and easily in the tones of the original speaker and often with good grammar. The second is produced with painful effort, and with many mistakes in grammar and word meanings. As with normal people learning a foreign language, autistic children find difficulty with the little linking words such as 'in', 'on', 'under', 'before' and 'because'. They may leave them out altogether, saying for example 'want dinner' 'go car shops'. Later on they may put them in sentences but use them wrongly, as in 'put cup in table', 'sit from chair'. One common mistake the children make is to confuse two words that are opposite in meaning, or else to use one word of the pair with its true and with its opposite meaning. Thus 'switch on light' may be a request to switch the light on or off depending on the circumstances. Often one can see that the child is using the word 'on' to say 'do something appropriate to the light' and that he has not grasped the precise meaning of 'on' and 'off'.

Words that usually occur in pairs are often confused. 'Brush' may be called 'comb', or 'sock' may be called 'shoe'. At first 'Mummy' and 'Daddy' may be misnamed. His general behaviour shows that this is not because the child does not know the difference. His problem is that he cannot call the proper word to mind quickly and easily and therefore he makes a verbal mistake.

The children often muddle the order of letters inside words, and may say 'accitt' for 'attic', 'diccifult' for 'difficult', 'pasghetti' for 'spaghetti'. The order of words in sentences may be reversed, for example 'put bed on blanket', 'have strawberry shake milk'. If you ask a child 'What will you put in the box?' he is quite likely to say 'cupboard', because he interprets what he hears as 'What will you put the box in?' Autistic children, even those few who make good progress in speaking, cannot use words flexibly, or to express subtle ideas. They tend to learn one meaning only for a word or a whole phrase, and stick to that. When the child first begins to understand, he hears his mother say 'Do you want a biscuit?' When he can speak, he too says 'Do you want a biscuit?' because that is the magic phrase which opens the biscuit tin. It sounds as if the child is calling himself 'you' instead of 'I'. (This is known technically as 'reversal of pronouns'.) Normal children may do this for a brief time but soon learn the proper use of pronouns. When you think about it it is not surprising that autistic children have these problems. The real mystery is how normal children learn to use the words correctly so quickly.

An autistic child may use a whole sentence to mean one thing only, because of the situation in which he first heard it. One child used to say 'Don't throw it out of the window' when he meant 'No.' The children tend to learn one name only for things, and therefore become confused if they hear, for example, the kitchen cooker called both a 'stove' and an 'oven'. It is easy to imagine their problems over words that can have two meanings, such as the noun 'sheet' (which might refer either to bed linen or to a piece of paper). If a mother says in conversation, 'I will meet you later on', her young autistic child may say 'Have meat dinner' with an expression of pleasure at having understood something at last.

The children have so little feeling for everyday speech that they can sound old-fashioned and pedantic, like the boy who said, 'May I extract a biscuit from the tin?' They tend to be literal and concrete. If asked 'What will you do when you get up from the table?' the answer is likely to be 'Stand on floor'. The speech of autistic children has been described as similar to that of a computer translating from a foreign language, and this does give an idea of the kinds of mistakes they tend to make.

iv *Poor pronunciation and voice control*

As I explained before, an autistic child may repeat phrases he hears from other people, with the correct pronunciation, accent and tone of voice that was used by the original speaker. When he tries to say things which he has thought out for himself his pronunciation may be very poor indeed. He has trouble with the same sounds that bother young normal children, such as 's' 'th' 'sh'. Autistic children often miss off the ends of words or use fragments of words – 'li' for 'lid' and 'bicle' for 'bicycle'. Some of them seem to have difficulty in distinguishing certain sounds they hear. They may confuse words that are rather similar, such as soup and soap, or else have trouble with telling the hard 'f' from the soft 'v' or the hard 'c' from the soft 'g'.

An autistic child usually has difficulty in controlling the loudness of his voice. He finds it hard to produce a smooth flow of speech, his voice goes up and down in the wrong places, and may have a mechanical quality. Many children go through a phase in which they say some things in a 'special' voice, different from their ordinary one. This may be a copy of something they have heard, but sometimes seems to be an attempt to try out different sounds.

All these problems mean that the children have to make an effort to speak. They try to get round this by making sentences as short as they can. 'Home after bread' is a good example, meaning 'Let's go home after we have bought the bread'. Normal people use many more words than are strictly necessary, while autistic children are more economical.

v *Problems in understanding things that are seen*

Autistic children have just as many problems with understanding things they see as with things they hear. I have already described how, as babies, they ignore many things which normal children enjoy looking at, whereas they may be fascinated by lights or shiny metal or paper. This lasts into childhood. They may also be distressed by extra bright lights, such as those used for photography.

When young, the children may look at something that moves but lose interest when the movement stops. They seem to recognise people and objects by their general outline rather than by details of their appearance. This suggests that the children may make most use of the part of the eye which attends to movement and outline, and have problems in using the part which perceives fine detail. Normal people use the movement-detecting part mostly in conditions of near darkness, when it is not possible to observe any detail. It is therefore interesting that some autistic children walk downstairs and even ride a tricycle without seeming to look where they are going, and may find their way in the dark quite as easily as in the light. A number of parents have noticed that their young autistic child may not bother to switch on the light if alone in a dark room, but can find his possessions and move around with no difficulty. A group of psychologists have shown that autistic children, unlike normal children, do not fix their gaze on people or objects for any length of time, but dart rapid glances and then look away. This gives the impression that the children deliberately avoid looking at other people's faces, especially their eyes, but tests have shown that they look comparatively longer at human faces than they do at anything else. The exception to this is when they are fascinated by something such as a piece of shiny paper. Then they will gaze fixedly for long periods of time.

Many of the children are late in showing any interest in pictures. When they do begin to look at picture books, they tend to pick out one small piece of the whole, such as a bar of chocolate in a picture of a sweet shop, probably because they cannot take in the meaning of the whole scene. Very complicated and rapidly changing environments like crowded shops may upset a young autistic child, and bring on a temper tantrum.

vi *Problems in understanding gestures*

People can communicate with each other in many ways other than talking. They use gestures, facial expressions and bodily movements. In a foreign country they may mime their needs or demonstrate with objects. Deaf people can lip read, or use finger talk, or write down what they want to say. All these methods involve using one's eyes and understanding what is seen. Autistic children, unlike deaf children, are handicapped in using even these 'visual' languages. In the first year or so the only 'language' they have is indiscriminate screaming. In the stage after this, they show their needs by grabbing someone by the hand, pulling him along, and putting his hand on the desired object. It may be years before a child begins to point, and then he usually uses his whole hand and does not point one finger. The children are unable to mime. An autistic child does not ask for a drink by putting an imaginary cup to his lips and pretending to swallow. Often the children have to be taught to use such simple gestures as a smile or a hug to welcome their parents.

They have as much trouble in understanding visual languages as in using them. As time goes on, however, especially if they develop the ability to look at things for a longer time, and to be more aware of details, they begin to have some comprehension of the meaning of clear, simple gestures and expressions. Usually they make faster progress with understanding (though not with using) visual than with spoken language, and may then appear to understand more of what is said than they really do, because they find clues in people's faces and movements.

vii *The senses of touch, taste and smell*

Parents and teachers soon notice that autistic children explore the world through their senses of touch, taste and smell, and that they do this long after the baby and toddler stage has passed. They love the feel of smooth wood, plastic or soft fur. The children often seem to recognise other people through these senses, and may like to smell their parents' hands and explore their faces with a soft delicate touch like that of a blind child. They enjoy rough games involving physical contact, although sometimes they will pull away from a more gentle touch or a kiss.

Although willing to explore things by tasting them,

some of the children have difficulty with learning to chew
lumpy food, and have to have their food mashed up for
them for considerably longer than normal. Young autistic
children can appear insensitive to cold and pain. They will
run out of doors with no clothes on in icy weather or ignore
knocks and bumps. This usually becomes less marked with
age and older children may be over-sensitive to discomfort.
Some children, especially those in institutions where there
is little occupation and supervision, may pick at sore places
or injure themselves in various ways such as biting or head
banging. These injuries may be severe although the child
appears to feel no pain.

viii *Unusual bodily movements*

One of the most noticeable things about an autistic
child is that he has many odd movements. He will flap
his arms and hands, jump up and down, and make facial
grimaces. He tends to walk on tiptoe, sometimes holding
his legs stiffly. A few of the children spin round and round
without becoming giddy. Nearly all of them twist and
turn their fingers or objects near their eyes.

These movements of hands, limbs and face are most
obvious when an autistic child is excited or is gazing at
something which has absorbed his whole attention, such
as a piece of string which he is twiddling in his fingers.
On the other hand, if he is occupied in some constructive
activity, the movements are hardly seen at all.

ix *Clumsiness in skilled movements*

One of the legends about autistic children is that they
are graceful in movement. As usual, the facts are more
complicated. Some autistic children are graceful when they
walk, and are able to climb and balance like cats. Other
children are rather clumsy and walk as if they have some

difficulty in balancing, and they usually do not enjoy climbing.

The children may be skilful and nimble with their fingers, or they may be stiff and clumsy. A child who is good with his hands may be poorly co-ordinated in his walking and running, or vice versa. Any combination is possible.

However, nearly all autistic children, whether they appear to be graceful or clumsy, are immature in the way they move. They often hold their arms awkwardly when they run, even when they have reached the age when normal children run with elbows bent and arms held close to their sides. They may climb the stairs by standing on each step in turn, when they should be old enough to alternate one foot on each stair. They tend to be late in reaching the stage of steadily swinging the arms when walking.

Many of these children hold their arms in a special way when unoccupied. They have their elbows bent and their hands near together in front of them, drooping at the wrists, with fingers slightly curled.

It is also common to find that autistic children have problems when they try to copy movements made by other people, even when they reach the stage at which they are willing to co-operate. They tend to do the reverse of the movement they see. That is, they will point down instead of up, and move the left arm instead of the right and so on. They usually cannot copy the movements of hopping on one foot, or skipping, and if they try an intricate dance step they become tangled up with their own feet.

This muddle about sequence and left-right, back-front and up-down affects many of their activities. I have already mentioned the tendency to mix the order of words in sentences. Some of the children, when they dress, tend to put clothes on back to front and shoes on the wrong feet. They lay the table with knives and forks on the wrong side and turn door handles in the wrong direction. If they begin to learn to read and write the letters of the alphabet, some autistic children confuse letters which are the reverse of each other, such as b and d, p and q, t and f, n and u and m and w.

DIFFICULT BEHAVIOUR AND EMOTIONAL PROBLEMS

Many people will feel that I should have started my description of autistic children with this section instead of putting it at the end. Behaviour difficulties are obvious and distressing in the early years, but there are good reasons, which I shall explain later, for believing that these problems follow from the children's inability to understand and cope with the world, and are not the first cause of their handicaps.

i *Aloofness and social withdrawal*

Most (though not all) young autistic children behave as though other people did not exist. It is possible to list the points in the behaviour of an autistic child which make him seem so aloof and distant – such a 'changeling child.' He does not come when he is called, he does not listen if you speak to him, his face may be empty of expression, he rarely looks straight at your face, he may pull away if you touch him, he does not put his arms round you if you pick him up, and he may walk past you (or over you, if you are sitting on the floor) without pausing in his stride. If he wants something he cannot reach for himself he grabs you by the back of your hand or wrist (not sliding his hand inside yours like a normal child) and pulls you along to do the work for him. Once he has the object you are ignored again. He shows no interest or sympathy if you are in pain or distress. He seems cut off, in a world of his own, completely absorbed in his own aimless activities.

However, the children do respond to adults who understand the handicaps and know how to break through the barriers these handicaps create. Then it is possible to see that the children have all the normal emotions, even if they are shown in very immature ways.

The children tend to become much more affectionate as they grow older. Sometimes when a child is five or six years old his mother feels that at last he is responding as he should have done when he was a baby.

ii *Resistance to change*

This problem may be shown in several different ways. Many of the children insist on repetition of the same routines. Paradoxically, when they are babies they may never settle to any routine of feeding or sleeping, but by the time they can walk they usually insist that certain things are done in precisely the same way every time. One child always wanted the same route for her daily walk, another insisted that the whole family kept to the same places at the table for every meal. A little boy would watch his mother lay the fire and become extremely upset if she did not place the paper, wood and coal in the same pattern every day. If the routine is upset there are screams and temper tantrums.

Some children have routines of their own, such as tapping on their chair before sitting down, standing up and turning round two or three times in the course of a meal, or placing objects in long lines.

Autistic children often become very attached to certain objects, and refuse to be parted from them. These may be ordinary toys like dolls or teddy bears, but often they are oddments such as pieces of string, holly leaves, tiny squares of photographic negative, or little bits of concrete. Some children are 'collectors' of such trifles as empty detergent packets, tins, plastic bottles, or dustpans. They will go to any lengths to add to their store. One little boy, when he realised he had to wait till detergent packets were empty, would throw away the powder from a full packet if it was left in his reach. Another child used to grab tins from displays in supermarkets, and would even run into people's houses to find old tins, if he was given the chance.

Resistance to change can apply to food, and though some autistic children have good appetites from the beginning, others go through a stage in which they refuse to eat more than two or three different things.

iii *Special fears*

It is quite common for the children to develop fears of harmless things, such as balloons, friendly dogs, or riding in buses. These fears can last for years, and may create difficulties for the whole family, especially if they are of common everyday objects or events which can hardly be avoided.

Conversely an autistic child can be unaware of real dangers, probably because he does not understand the possible consequences. One boy liked the sound of squealing car brakes and would dash in front of cars to make them brake sharply and thus produce this (to him) delightful noise.

Some autistic children are continually tense and frightened while others seem unconcerned and take things as they come. A child may change as he grows older, usually in the direction of becoming more relaxed. The differences are probably due to each child's own personality which determines the way he reacts to his handicaps.

iv *Socially embarrassing behaviour*

Since autistic children are limited in their understanding

of words, and are generally immature, they often behave in ways which are socially unacceptable. Some of them are quiet and rather passive children and do not cause much trouble, but others are energetic and determined, and, especially in the years between two and five, their parents have to cope with an endless series of awful situations.

An autistic child who is given to screaming is not inhibited by being in a public place, and will scream as loud and long in the street as at home. He may take things off shop counters, run into the back premises of shops, or enter the homes of complete strangers. He has no idea that it is not done to take off one's clothes in public and will happily disrobe to sit in an inviting puddle of rain water, if so inclined. He will rub his face against a fur coat, and look right through the person wearing it if she speaks to him. His table manners may leave much to be desired, and most of the children will happily pick up any food they drop on the floor and eat it, regardless of any dirt that may be collected at the same time.

The children who learn to talk at least a little become much better behaved in general, but even they cause small social crises. They do not understand that some things are better left unsaid. They may talk about topics that are not mentioned in polite society. Innocently, they make remarks about other people which may be hurtful. One girl who spoke very well, on seeing an unusually short woman, said, in her loud, clear voice, 'Mummy, look at that *dear* little lady'. Just like young normal children, autistic children tend to pick up bad language and terms of abuse and bring them out on most unsuitable occasions.

Autistic children never tell lies. They do not understand why it should ever be necessary to avoid the truth, and in any case lack the skill with language and ideas needed to invent lies. Their naivety leads to a devastating lack of awareness of social conventions, or of other people's feelings.

v *Inability to play*

Normal children learn about the world through play. They begin by exploring the feel, taste and smell of different objects, but as they develop language and an understanding of the world around them they gradually begin to use toys to represent real things. They stop throwing the toy train on the floor to hear the noise it makes and start pretending that it will take them for a ride. They stop chewing the doll's foot and begin to cuddle it (the right way up), to dress it, to scold it – in short to pretend that the doll is a baby.

Autistic children have problems with all kinds of language, and their ability to play suffers in consequence. To them a toy train is not a pretend real train – it is just an object which is cold, hard, green, heavy, has a metallic taste and rattles when you shake it and makes funny patterns to look at when the wheels are spun. The children explore all objects, whether they are toys or discarded rubbish, in order to experience the simple sensations which give them great pleasure. As far as play is concerned, they remain at the stage of the baby who is just beginning to be able to hold things in his hands.

Most autistic children will play with water, sand or mud for hours on end (although a few of them have an intense dislike of becoming wet or dirty). They enjoy watching patterns of movement, and some become remarkably skilful at spinning coins or other objects. As they grow older, a number of the children are able to do jigsaws and similar puzzles, although they often fit the pieces by feel and not because of the clues from the pictures. They may also like constructional toys, although they are not really interested in the finished object but simply in the pleasure of fitting the pieces together.

Lacking language and imagination, they cannot join

in other children's games. When young they ignore other children, but they may reach the stage when they want to take part but do not know how. Even the autistic children who have quite high intelligence are limited in their leisure activities. It is a common complaint of the parents of this kind of child that, although he is able to paint, or draw or play the piano, he has to be pushed into practising these skills, and seems to prefer unconstructive activity such as listening to the same record over and over again, or doing nothing at all.

SPECIAL SKILLS

So far, I have talked about autistic children's handicaps, but one of the surprising things is that some of them have special skills at which they perform well. This gives parents the feeling that their children would be completely normal if only the key to the puzzle could be found – if only something would 'make the penny drop'. Most of the children love music and rhythmic sounds. Some can sing well even at an early age, a few can play some musical instrument, and there are a smaller number still who are able to compose music.

The children can usually learn to use numbers more easily than words. Some of them are able to do long sums in their heads at great speed. They often like mechanical toys, and some learn to operate the radio and record player long before they learn to talk.

Many of the children are handicapped in drawing because of their problems with understanding the things they see. They draw strange-looking figures to represent human beings. Others who are more advanced may be able to draw and paint well, although they nearly always copy things they see or remember from the past, and are not creative.

Parents often notice that the children know at once if

any of their special collections are disturbed in any way. They seem to recognise each pebble or piece of wood, even if to grown-up eyes one item is just like the other ninety-nine. The children may also be able to find their way back to places after one visit and know where objects of special interest (to them) are to be found in houses they have not visited for years.

None of these special abilities depends on language. Music, numbers, and memory for places are dealt with by different parts of the brain from those concerned with speech. There are stories about autistic children who could recite long poems or lists of names, but being able to learn like a parrot is not the same as being able to use language normally and fluently.

The general rule is that the children perform better at skills which do not need language. These activities are their main source of enjoyment in life.

CHANGES AFTER FIVE YEARS OF AGE

Parents of autistic children have a hard time in the early years. The children's behaviour is so difficult, and progress seems so slow that their parents almost lose hope of any improvement. It is some comfort for them to know that, in general, there tends to be a distinct change for the better around five to seven years of age. This does not always happen. Some autistic children remain difficult, but the majority do improve at least to some extent after the first few years.

The biggest change is usually in the social and emotional problems. The children become more affectionate and sociable, less resistant to change, less given to needless fears but more aware of real danger, and better behaved in public. Their language problems and difficulties with movements also become less marked, but change in these areas is not so great as for general behaviour.

This improvement can create problems in diagnosis, since most writers describe autistic children as they are at their worst. When seeing older children, it is particularly important for the doctor to ask parents to give all the details they can about their child's behaviour in the early years.

5

Theories of causes

There are, in general, two main kinds of theories. One says that autistic children are normal when they are born, but that their emotional development is disturbed because of the way they are brought up. A special variant of this is that autistic children have the wrong kind of learning experiences from the time they are born, and are 'conditioned' into abnormal behaviour.

The other kind of theory suggests that autistic children have some physical abnormality in their brain that makes them behave in the way they do.

Parents, quite naturally, are inclined to resent the emotional theories, because however carefully the explanations are worded, the parents feel they are being blamed. Indignation and a refusal to be browbeaten into guilt are healthy reactions, but it is also necessary to consider the evidence as carefully as possible and to understand the basis for these ideas.

THEORIES WHICH SUGGEST EMOTIONAL CAUSES

There are three main reasons for the belief in an emotional cause. Firstly, most autistic children, when they are young, have many behaviour problems including a striking difficulty in relating to other people and in showing affection. Secondly, when Professor Kanner first wrote about the children, most psychiatrists were enthusiastic about the importance of early childhood experiences in producing every kind of mental illness. The climate of opinion at the time favoured the argument from emotional symptoms to emotional causes.

Thirdly, various writers said that they had found that parents of these children had abnormal personalities. Some said the mothers were cold and hard and rejected their babies. Others said the mothers overprotected and smothered their babies. Professor Kanner and his colleagues said the mothers were not especially abnormal but that the fathers were odd, being over-intellectual, rigid, detached, humourless – dedicated to their professions rather than to their children.

The first two reasons are less convincing nowadays, because people have become aware that children who are handicapped in understanding the world for any reason usually have emotional problems as a secondary consequence. Also many psychiatrists and psychologists are not quite so certain of the emotional causes of all mental illness.

With regard to parents' personalities, the early workers (and some recent ones too) described their personal impressions which could easily have been biased. Furthermore, in discussions of this subject, some people separate autistic children from other psychotic children, while others do not. There have been only a very small number of studies which tried to use scientific methods to compare a group of parents of autistic children with parents of other handicapped and of normal children. They produced no evidence that parents of autistic children were especially abnormal, apart from the tendency to higher intelligence than the average, although they did have the same problems as parents of any other kind of handicapped child. These studies were by no means perfect, but they were better planned than most of the previous work.

The fact that the parents of autistic children are likely to be more intelligent, better educated and of higher occupational level than average has also been used as an argument to say that they are uninterested in their children, and treat them too objectively. The few studies with control groups did not prove that the parents were detached from their children, and one showed that the parents of autistic children were more involved with their handicapped child than the parents of mongol children. Furthermore, while it is possible for parents to have more than one autistic child, in most cases the brothers and sisters are healthy and normal.

Finally, no one has ever shown that orphanages or institutions which give no 'mothering' to their babies, and where the staff have no time for baby-talk, produce autistic children.

THEORIES WHICH SUGGEST PHYSICAL CAUSES

Many people now think that a physical cause (also called an 'organic' cause) is most probable. They point to the fact that about one-third of all autistic children have other abnormalities of the brain and nervous system as well as their autism. They observe the many problems that the children have in understanding and using any kind of language, and their difficulties in co-ordination of skilled movements which closely resemble those found in other conditions known to have a physical cause.

One worker X-rayed a group of autistic children and found that the maturing of their bones was delayed. They may be physically immature in other ways and tend to keep their childish features and soft babyish hands longer than most children, although puberty occurs in the average age range. Unusual sleeping patterns are common. Many of the children seem to need much less sleep than most normal children. They may lie awake till 11 or 12 at night, and wake again at 6 a.m., but do not seem to be tired in the day.

Finally, doctors and psychologists who favour a physical cause generally feel that the parents they have met are an average cross-section of humanity, apart from their tendency to higher intelligence. This shows how difficult it is to rely upon subjective judgments made without proper methods of measurement. It seems hard on parents that the early theories of parental abnormality were put forward without any scientific proof, and have caused much unhappiness ever since.

Research workers who are investigating the possible physical causes of early childhood autism are working along several different lines. Some are interested in possible basic causes, such as an inherited abnormality, or an injury, infection, of some other harmful event, occurring before, during or after birth. Methods of studying these problems include examining detailed family histories, looking at the chromosomes of the children and their relatives, and finding out if problems during pregnancy, birth and early childhood are particularly common in autistic children.

Even if it were possible to decide the basic cause (or causes), further questions still have to be answered. The next step is to ask how does the abnormal gene, or the harmful event, produce its effect? Does it affect the brain directly, or indirectly through some abnormality of the body's chemistry? Ways of answering this question include studies of the biochemistry of the body, and special neurological examinations.

The third set of questions in the series is, what part of the brain is involved, and how does this affect the child's behaviour? These are just as difficult to answer as the other problems. Methods of examining the way the brain is working are still unsatisfactory. In conditions like early childhood autism, research workers have to watch the children's behaviour, observe their handicaps, and then argue back to what might be going on in the brain. It is not surprising that there is considerable disagreement on this subject.

'Brain damage' has been put forward as the cause, but this is a general term which does not explain very much, because children given this label may have many different patterns of behaviour. Most workers have tried to be more specific when explaining childhood autism. A few have suggested that the parts of the brain which control the emotions are abnormal. Several research groups feel that the areas which deal with waking and sleeping (the 'reticular system') do not function properly. Others believe that the problem lies in the parts of the brain which deal with organisation of information coming in through the senses, and the understanding of language (verbal and non-verbal).

The last idea has been worked out in more detail in the theory of 'multiple language handicaps'. This suggests that autistic children have a number of different abnormalities which add together to give them a severe language problem. Thus, some of the abnormalities affect responses to sound and understanding of spoken speech; others affect the children's ability to understand the things they see; some interfere with the ability to use and understand gestures; some affect the ability to copy complicated movements, and therefore make it difficult for the children to learn to express themselves in their bodily postures and activities.

Each one of these abnormalities can occur alone, or combined with abnormalities which are not especially characteristic of autistic children. When this happens there is usually much argument about the 'true' diagnosis because the child concerned will resemble an autistic child in some ways and not in others. Each abnormality by itself will affect some aspect of the ability to communicate with other people, and will lead to some social and behavioural difficulties. When they are all added together as they are in an autistic child, the behaviour problems are multiplied and affect every aspect of life. The children have no way of understanding the world or of communicating, so it is small wonder that they appear aloof and isolated, that they cling on desperately to the few things they do understand, that they are fearful but do not appreciate real danger, and that their behaviour is immature and unpredictable.

Autistic children (although their eyes and ears are usually normal) are in a similar situation to a child who is born partially blind and partially deaf and who also has difficulty in comprehending the little speech he can hear. Very rarely, children are born with these handicaps because their mothers had German measles at an early stage in pregnancy, and some of them behave as if they had early childhood autism. This could be predicted from the 'multiple language handicap' theory.

Autistic children differ from each other in the severity of their handicaps. There are children who have a number but not all of the typical symptoms. As the children grow older some of the problems may improve more than others. These findings also fit with the theory.

The chances are that a number of different pathological processes could affect the parts of the brain that are important for human communication, and produce the same effects on behaviour.

Most people feel that eventually many causes will be found, each accounting for one sub-group of children who are at present classified together. Perhaps the absolutely typical autistic children described by Professor Kanner will be found to form one group with one cause, but even that is not yet certain.

Some people think that the handicaps of autistic children result from a severe delay in some aspects of normal development. Others believe that the children have definite abnormalities – that they are in certain important ways different from normal children, and not simply lagging behind. This interesting question is still unsolved, but the latest work on language development may eventually provide some of the answers.

6

Comparisons with other childhood handicaps and problems

DIFFICULT PHASES IN NORMAL CHILDREN

Everything that an autistic child does, normal children may do at some time or other during their development. Normal children have problems while learning to talk and to read and write; they sometimes take no notice when spoken to; they may ignore other people; they have temper tantrums; they may hold on to a piece of rag or a teddy bear and weep when it is lost; they have their special fears, and they sometimes seem oblivious of danger. The difference is that in a normal child these things happen in passing phases, whereas they continue for years on end in an autistic child. Also, normal children have a wide range of interests and activities, while autistic children are limited and repetitive in the things they do. When they are seen together, the contrast between a normal and an autistic child is painfully obvious.

CONGENITAL DEAFNESS

Children who are born deaf have many problems in learning to understand and use spoken language. They may be socially withdrawn and difficult in their behaviour and have various symptoms seen in autistic children, especially when young. However, they are able to learn gestures, miming, lip-reading and finger language. They use their eyes to compensate for their lack of hearing.

A C.—D

It is important to make sure that children with autistic behaviour are not deaf. Testing is often a difficult problem, but the parents' observations of their child's behaviour at home can be most helpful in making a decision.

As explained in the previous section, some children born both deaf and blind behave like autistic children. The diagnosis depends on the history and physical examination.

CONGENITAL APHASIA

Children with congenital aphasia have problems with spoken language. Those with 'receptive' aphasia have severe difficulty in understanding words, and therefore in learning to speak. Children with 'executive' aphasia can understand reasonably well but have difficulty in producing words for themselves. The children with receptive aphasia are especially likely to be confused with autistic children when young because they too tend to ignore sounds and to be socially withdrawn. The children with executive aphasia are usually more responsive and sociable but they have the same problem as autistic children in copying movements made by other people and in speaking. Both groups of aphasic children differ from autistic children in that they use their eyes to help them understand the world, and they communicate well in non-verbal ways.

It is possible to find aphasic children with extra handicaps who are very similar to autistic children. Receptive and executive aphasia often occur in association with early childhood autism. Aphasia and autism shade into each other and it is often hard to tell in which group to place a particular child. A description of each child's handicaps is therefore more use than giving him a single diagnostic label.

VISUAL PROBLEMS

Children may have visual problems because of conditions

affecting the eyes, or the nerves from the eyes to the brain, or the parts of the brain receiving messages from the eyes. Sometimes, depending on the cause and the nature of the handicap, children with visual problems may have the same kinds of hand movements, and the same tendency to jump and spin round as autistic children. They may even be very concerned about routines and become most unhappy if anything in the house is moved from its usual place. They may appear to look past or through other people, and their social behaviour may be a problem. It is usually possible to tell the difference between autistic children and children with visual problems alone, because the latter do not have the same difficulties with understanding the things they hear. The history and physical examination also give the diagnosis.

MENTAL RETARDATION

This is a general label which covers a large number of different conditions. To give just a few examples, retardation may be due to mongolism; microcephaly (a very small head and brain); phenylketonuria (a condition in which the body cannot cope with certain kinds of food, so that chemicals build up in the blood stream and affect the brain); inflammation of the brain in early life; or brain injury around the time of birth. The majority of retarded children, even though they are slow to mature, do not behave like autistic children. On the other hand a minority of them show some aspects of autistic behaviour, suggesting that they have one or more of the handicaps found in autistic children. This may happen with phenylketonuria, for example.

Some autistic children do well on intelligence tests that do not need language, but most of them are below average in intelligence and many are severely retarded because the handicaps which underlie autism produce serious learning problems. There are children who have early childhood autism together with some other condition which, by itself, would cause profound mental retardation. These children are the most handicapped of all, because they have no language and no non-verbal or physical skills either.

ELECTIVE MUTISM

A very small number of children talk in one situation (for example at home) but remain silent elsewhere (for example at school). This is fairly common in toddlers when first beginning to speak, but if it goes on until school age it is a cause for concern. Children with 'elective mutism', as it is called, may have a variety of speech and behaviour problems, but the pattern of their behaviour is different from that of an autistic child. The diagnosis has to be made by considering all the symptoms together, and not just the fact that the child is silent in some places. One of the most important distinguishing features is that the child with elective mutism can use speech and gestures fairly fluently when he does talk, and does not have the kind of speech disorders that occur in childhood autism.

OTHER TYPES OF CHILDHOOD PSYCHOSES

Early childhood autism is only one of the conditions which can be loosely grouped together as 'childhood psychoses'. Since autism is diagnosed from the special behaviour pattern, the distinction from other childhood psychoses depends upon a detailed history, and careful observation of behaviour. Some psychotic children are able to speak fluently and grammatically, but produce many strange and fantastic ideas. This in itself would rule out a diagnosis of early childhood autism, in which poor language development is a key symptom.

As interest in autistic children has increased in the last few years, people have started to consider this diagnosis every time they meet a handicapped child with rather unusual behaviour, or even an otherwise normal child who is quiet and shy. It is better to use the diagnosis as strictly as possible, confining it to children with most or all of the typical behaviour. If some people use the term very widely, and include all kinds of difficult children, it becomes impossible to judge the results of any methods of education or treatment which they may describe.

From the point of view of parents and children, the label of autism implies serious handicaps, and it is not in a child's best interests to make the diagnosis unless there are good reasons.

Part II
Education and management

Autistic children's handicaps are severe, they affect all the activities of daily living, and they are usually lifelong, though tending to a slow improvement. There is no known cure for these handicaps, but this does not mean that nothing can be done. The children can be helped to find ways round their difficulties with special methods of education, both at home and at school. In many ways the problem is similar to that faced by the parents and teachers of deaf or blind children. It may not be possible to cure the handicaps, but the children can be taught to make the best use of the skills they do possess. Some of the children have too many additional handicaps to make much progress, but even in these cases it is worth trying to improve the worst behaviour problems and to teach simple self-care.

7

What doctors can do

When parents first realise that there is something wrong with their child, they desperately hope that doctors will be able to make him better. They go to their first appointment with high expectations, which are bound to be disappointed. Sometimes they feel anger and bitterness against the doctor himself, and perhaps seek advice from one clinic after another. This is a waste of time and may even be harmful for the family if the parents never come to terms with reality. The problem is made worse by the fact that parents are likely to meet many different theories on their travels, and they become confused and depressed. Occasionally they even meet with professional workers who at first believe that they can *cure* the child with psychological treatment. After a varying period of time it becomes obvious that this is not going to happen. The therapist may decide to discontinue the treatment, and the parents feel let down, and that their child has been rejected once again.

It requires considerable courage for parents to make their own decision as to whom to trust and whose advice to follow. They usually have to make such a decision on the grounds of their own common sense and experience with children. They are fortunate if they can meet a number of other parents of older autistic children and find out for themselves which ideas have proved useful.

Doctors and parents can work together best if parents have reasonable expectations of how much the doctor can do.

DIAGNOSIS

Making sure of the diagnosis is the doctor's first task. He has to study the child's past history and behaviour and decide how far the pattern fits that of early childhood autism. He then goes on to find out if the child has any of the conditions which can be mistaken for autism. In particular he has to satisfy himself that the child is not deaf, and has no difficulty with seeing.

The next step is to consider if the child has any associated handicaps. These might be abnormalities of the brain and nervous system such as spasticity or fits, or he might have some other physical problem which adds to his difficulties. Doctors have to be especially careful in assessing these extra handicaps, because the child cannot complain for himself and his odd behaviour might hide symptoms and signs that would be obvious in a normal child.

A detailed diagnosis takes time, and needs trust and co-operation between the doctor and his assistants on the one side, and the family on the other.

DISCUSSION WITH PARENTS

I have put this near the top of the list of the things that doctors can do, because a full and frank discussion as soon as possible after the parents realise that the child is handicapped can have a positive effect upon their whole attitude to the problem in the future.

Most parents like to be given a name for what is wrong with their child, but the sensible doctor does not leave it at that. He can explain to the parents how their child is handicapped. For example he can tell them that their little boy can understand simple instructions but not complicated ones, and that he has problems in pronunciation. He can let the parents know about the child's difficulties in comprehending the things he sees, and how all these handicaps upset his emotions and his behaviour. A detailed analysis of this kind is much more helpful than giving the child a label.

The parents also want to know about the prospects for the future. They will appreciate it if they are told the truth. They need to know that the handicaps are long-lasting, but also that they, as parents, can do an enormous amount to help their child if they set about it in the right way.

It is a hard task for a doctor to have to tell parents that they have a severely handicapped child. A doctor in this situation has to deal with his own emotions as well as those of the parents, and it requires all his skill, experience, and human compassion to handle the situation successfully, and to build a basis for a co-operative effort throughout the long years ahead.

TREATMENT OF ADDITIONAL HANDICAPS

The more handicaps a child has, the harder he finds it to cope with life. It is therefore important to make sure that an autistic child is as physically fit as possible. Sometimes it is difficult to give special treatment when the child is young (such as exercises for spasticity, or glasses for poor vision) but efforts can be made at intervals, and the full procedures started as soon as he is at the stage when he can co-operate, or at least not fight against the efforts to help him.

Routine physical care, such as inoculations, dental care, and treatment for childish illnesses, is often a problem. Suggestions for parents will be given in the next section, but doctors and dentists can do their work more effectively if they get to know the child and obtain his trust before he needs any medical or dental care.

Having to wait a long time to be seen is a strain for a handicapped child. It is also hard on the parents and the

other patients if the child's behaviour becomes disturbed.
The understanding doctor or dentist tries to arrange appointments to avoid this problem, if the circumstances make
this possible.

ALLEVIATION OF SECONDARY BEHAVIOUR PROBLEMS

Medical methods are sometimes useful for relieving special
problems. One example is sleeplessness, especially when
the child keeps the whole family awake every night because
of his screaming. If nothing else works, the doctor may
prescribe sleeping tablets as a temporary measure. Tablets
of this kind must never be given without a doctor's advice.
This is a good general rule, but it is particularly important
where autistic children are concerned. They may be resistant
to normal doses of sedatives, and sometimes drugs can
excite a child instead of calming him down.

Overactivity and restlessness can sometimes be helped by
drugs prescribed by a doctor. In general it is better to try
to improve the child's behaviour through sensible management, because drugs have undesirable side effects and in
any case may not produce the desired result. There are
times, however, when medication has to be tried.

HELP WITH PLANNING AN EDUCATIONAL PROGRAMME

Doctors can help parents and teachers to plan a programme
of education, by telling them the details of the child's
handicaps. Examples of ways in which this knowledge can
be used will be given in the next sections.

Passing on information should be a continuing and a
two-way process. Parents and teachers are with the children
for many hours each day and are in a position to observe
behaviour that a doctor can never see in a brief office visit.
Evaluation of the child's handicaps and the progress he is

making can be done most effectively if all the available information is brought together in regular discussions.

PSYCHOTHERAPY

Psychotherapy and even psychoanalysis have been attempted with autistic children, but there is no evidence that they are effective in curing or even diminishing the children's handicaps. This is not surprising since psychotherapeutic techniques presuppose the development of language and the ability to symbolise, and these are the skills which autistic children conspicuously lack. The use of psychotherapeutic techniques which encourage 'regression' (for example, bottle feeding a child of seven to encourage him to go back to the baby stage and 'start again') seems particularly inappropriate for autistic children. The theory is that the child has to be returned to the stage before his development went wrong, and that he will then be able to 'begin again' and will develop normally. However there is no scientific evidence that these techniques are helpful. The most successful methods are those which try to help the child move forward in development, rather than backward. Sometimes older children who have made good progress and who are able to talk fairly well become unhappily aware that they are different from others of their age. Such a child could be helped by psychotherapy from someone who understood his handicaps. Autistic children, like normal children, may be depressed by the loss of someone they love and depend upon, and by other major crises of life, and may need the help of someone experienced in this kind of work.

Professional workers who hold theories which imply that the parents 'cause' their child to become autistic may recommend that these parents should have psychotherapy or psychoanalysis, in order to help the child indirectly. There is no evidence that this is useful in practice.

On the whole parents find that their emotional distress is lessened as they begin to understand what is wrong with their child, and, even more important, what they can do to help him. Some families find they can accept a handicapped child fairly easily, and come to terms with their unhappiness as time goes on. Others are less philosophical, for many different personal reasons. Some of these parents may want and benefit from psychotherapy given by someone who understands what it means to have a child who is different. The aim should be to lessen any tendency to morbid self-blame, and release the parents' energies for the task in hand.

8

What teachers can do

This book is written for parents, and is not intended to give details of methods of education. All I shall do is to mention the important role which teachers play in helping autistic children to achieve their full potential.

A teacher's task is easier if an autistic child has reasonable social behaviour, if he can feed, wash and dress himself and is clean and dry in the day time, but she often has to begin by teaching these skills.

Once this basic behaviour has been established, the teacher can go on to other things. Teaching methods have to be adapted to the children's handicaps, and utilise many of the techniques used with blind, deaf and aphasic children. Montessori equipment is good because much of it gives the children the opportunity of using touch and movement for learning. All the ways of teaching I shall mention in the next section are used in specialist schools – that is, teaching motor skills by guiding the child's limbs, helping learning by the proper use of encouragement and discouragement, and, for the more advanced children, the use of pictures, diagrams and models to get across an idea without depending solely upon words.

The subjects taught in special schools include those which can be found in the normal school curriculum such as reading, writing, arithmetic, music, art, cooking, sewing and other domestic work, wood work and metal work. The difference is that most schools for autistic children cater for a wide range of abilities, so some children will be able to achieve only a few simple skills, while a few can move on to wider subjects. The majority, somewhere between the two ends of the scale, are very handicapped in learning, but their school experience improves their ability to cope with life. Good teachers know from experience when to watch and wait, and when to apply some pressure to ensure that a child moves forward in learning. They know how to make the best use of the improvement which occurs as a child grows and matures so that no opportunity is lost. One important aspect of school is that it provides a structured environment and experience of social mixing. School outings, birthday and Christmas parties and the daily assembly of the whole school, give a rhythm and pattern to life which the children find both comforting and stimulating. The most successful schools, once they are well established, develop a tradition of reasonable behaviour which is a great asset. Even the most disturbed children become calmer and more co-operative when introduced into such an atmosphere. Teachers find that autistic children are considerably influenced by these social pressures, even though they appear to ignore the other children. It is impressive to observe the social competence that can be acquired in the right kind of school. Children who appeared confused and lost can learn to find their way around the school with confidence, and carry out all the small routines with calm assurance.

A teacher is one member of the team which should be concerned in helping an autistic child. She has to work with doctors and psychologists, as a professional with her own expertise, but willing to use the knowledge and advice provided by experts in other fields. She needs to have knowledge and experience of normal child development and of teaching normal children, so that she can recognise the stages in the progress of an autistic child, and not mistake immature behaviour for a pathological symptom. She is also an important person for the parents. She can learn a lot about the children in her care by listening to the parents' account of the behaviour at home. Methods of management which have been found to work at school and at home can be exchanged, and problems and possible solutions discussed. A parent-teacher association provides an excellent opportunity for co-operation between home and school. A teacher is sometimes in a particularly good position to help parents who have lost heart, and who do not know how to help their own child. If the teacher can help him to make progress the parents may be able to find fresh courage and to learn from her success.

One thing that teachers and parents have to avoid is jealousy over who can manage the child best. Both home and school play their own special parts in the plan for helping the child. The roles are different but complementary and both are of equal value. Problems can also arise if teachers try to assume the role of psychotherapists for the child, the parents or the whole family. The teachers' real skills are too important to be hampered by attempting to mix them with those of a different discipline.

9

What parents can do

AUTISTIC BABIES

Autism is usually not diagnosed until the age of two or later, so no one can recommend well-tried and -tested ways of dealing with problems in babies who are going to be autistic children. Parents usually look back regretfully to the early days, and think how much better they would have managed if only they had understood what was wrong.

SOCIAL INTERACTION

It seems reasonable to suggest that, if a baby seems unresponsive, his mother should make a special effort to cuddle him, tickle him, carry him around and talk to him, so that he has the same experiences as a normal baby. The relationship between a mother and a normal baby is built up by each responding to the other. The baby depends on his mother to play with him and caress him, so that he can learn to be sociable and come to realise how important she is to him. On the other hand, a mother needs her baby to show his pleasure in her company, by cooing, chuckling, wriggling with delight and making himself ready to be picked up. An autistic baby who seems aloof and self-contained misses out on these vital early interactions with his mother, not because she is abnormal, but because he is handicapped.

A mother with this kind of baby has to be encouraged to do all the work herself, and she is usually only too happy to do this, once she realises that she will not harm the baby by breaking into his isolation.

BABY TALK

The baby's lack of interest in his mother's baby-talk tends to make her talk less and less, until she says as little to him as he does to her. Again, explanation and encouragement are needed so that she chats to the baby even if he takes no notice. Many mothers remember that their autistic children liked having words whispered right into their ear. This makes sense, because experts in the way children develop language point out that babies learn to talk on their mothers' laps, hearing their mothers' voice while in close physical contact. Whispering into the baby's ear brings mother and child even closer, and adds pleasant physical sensations as well.

Another way of getting an autistic child's attention is to sing to him. Baby talk and simple sentences can be sung to tunes he likes, and his first word may be the last word of the line of a nursery rhyme.

SLEEPLESSNESS AND SCREAMING

If the baby screams regularly every night for some hours, it may be helpful for the parents to arrange between them to have one night looking after the baby and one night sleeping. Loss of sleep can be extremely wearing, and help from a relative or a children's nurse may be the only solution to give the parents a few nights' unbroken sleep. It is important that the child should meet a new night-nurse in his mother's company, and in the day time before she takes charge for the night. If this is not arranged, the sudden appearance of a stranger can make the child even more disturbed than usual.

It is worth while trying different ideas to see if a sleepless screaming baby can be helped to settle. Some babies like to have a light left on. One little boy would sleep peacefully only if he were wrapped up tightly in a sheet, like a little cocoon. The old-fashioned remedy of rocking sometimes works. A few parents have had to give their baby sedatives, under the supervision of a doctor, since this was the only way to break a habit of sleepless nights which had gone on for many months.

AUTISTIC CHILDREN

Once babyhood has passed, and the child can walk, the pattern of autistic behaviour becomes obvious. The diagnosis is usually made around this time, and parents have to begin the long process of helping their child to fit into the family and the world. The problems they meet during the years of childhood are many and varied, and each child has his own special difficulties as well as those which are common to most of the children. All I can do here is to write about some of the situations with which parents have to cope, and to make some suggestions based on ideas which have proven helpful in practice.

In the early years when the children have few, if any, means of communication, the management of difficult behaviour is the first priority. Later on, as communication develops, behaviour is less difficult, and the main problems are teaching the skills of living and trying to stimulate the children's interest in constructive activities.

MANAGING DIFFICULT BEHAVIOUR

Having a disturbed child makes most people feel that they are miserable failures as parents, even though the other children in the family may behave quite normally. The thing to remember is that the ordinary methods of bringing up children, based largely on the supposition that the child understands what you say to him, do not work with autistic children. Parents cannot help making mistakes because they naturally act towards the child as if he were normal, right up until the time when they begin to understand why he is so different.

In general, parents and teachers need to discourage disturbed behaviour and to encourage constructive, socially acceptable behaviour. Normal babies and children learn in a number of different ways. Firstly, early on, they become aware of their mother's tone of voice, the expression on her face, small nods or shakes of her head, the way she stands and moves, all of which show whether she is approving or disapproving. Secondly, as soon as they begin to understand the words they hear, normal children can learn through speech as well as gestures. Thirdly, they also imitate their parents as best they can within the limits of their understanding.

None of these ways is particularly rapid or efficient in the very young child, because his capacity to understand has to grow and mature, so in an emergency a parent has to use a more direct method of teaching. If a baby crawls towards a boiling kettle, his mother does not rely on gestures, words, or his ability to imitate in order to prevent an accident. Instead, she grabs him as soon as she realises what he intends to do, and she continues to prevent him from scalding himself even if he becomes annoyed and tearful. Similarly a mother instinctively uses direct physical methods (such as hugging and kissing) to show her approval when her baby has done something which pleases her. She knows that words and gestures are not enough by themselves, although she uses them as well.

The problem with a young autistic child is that the first three ways of learning are closed to him because of his language handicaps, and only the last way is available. With the development of language, normal children begin to be able to remember and to anticipate. They can understand if they are warned not to behave in a certain way, and if they are scolded after they have been naughty. As they mature, this capacity to look both backward and forward in time increases, until finally a normal adult can plan for years in the future. Autistic children, until they develop some ability to communicate, are bound by the present. They link things that happen at the same time, or very close in time, whether this is justified or not, and they are unable to appreciate the connection between two events which are a few minutes apart. It is all too easy for these children to make mistakes about how things link together, as I shall describe in the discussion of 'special fears'.

Recently, a number of psychologists have become interested in the direct methods of learning which are useful with children and adults with limited comprehension of language. The techniques they have developed are known as 'operant conditioning' or 'behaviour modification'. These methods have been discussed widely in the popular press as well as in scientific journals, and sometimes they have received adverse publicity and strong criticism. This is firstly because some workers have used harsh ways of discouraging undesirable behaviour; secondly because 'conditioning' appears to mean a detached, scientific approach to bringing up children; and thirdly because of the possibility that behaviour learnt under special concentrated conditions may not generalise to everyday life in the school, or at home with the family.

These objections are still being debated in the scientific literature on learning theory. However, some of the basic principles are accepted by almost everyone, and fit well into a general programme of child-rearing and education. Parents and teachers can borrow the most useful techniques from the specialists, and apply them to suit their own children. In a few places, mostly in the USA, professional workers provide special teaching for parents to enable them to help their children in their own homes. This most promising idea is beginning to arouse interest in many centres concerned with handicapped children. It is worth noting that people who are intuitively good with children have always made use of many of the ideas which the psychologists have had to work out from long laborious studies.

The first step is to try to understand why a child behaves in a particular way. It is helpful to remember that the behaviour of an autistic child, though it often appears to be bizarre and strange, always has a concrete logical reason behind it. By this, I mean that it is the simple response of a handicapped child faced with a complex situation which he does not understand. It is not the expression of inner fantasies, because these depend on the comprehension and use of some kind of symbolic language.

The studies of methods of changing behaviour have confirmed the obvious, in that they have shown that children tend to repeat behaviour which in the past has led to reward, and to stop behaving in ways that are not rewarded.

When dealing with a child who cannot speak and who cannot understand very much, it is vital to time things so that you react *at once* to reward or to discourage. The best thing is to act to prevent bad behaviour, or if that cannot be done, to take action as soon as the behaviour starts. This is more likely to work than allowing a child to do something naughty or dangerous, and then punishing him afterwards. It seems that if he has already had the fun of doing the forbidden act, the punishment counts for little. Many parents find that their child is not deterred by being smacked after he has done something wrong. He may even laugh, or cheerfully anticipate the slap as a routine consequence of certain actions. Psychologists say that in this situation the slap acts, in a curious way, as a reward. Another problem is that children with poor comprehension of speech easily become confused about the reasons why their parents show disapproval. If you threaten to 'tell Daddy when he comes home', the child will have completely forgotten the reason a few moments later, and all he will learn is that Daddy is a person who often becomes very cross when he arrives home. This will make him unhappy about his father but will have no effect at all on his difficult behaviour.

To be effective, you must act quickly *every time* the child begins to show the difficult behaviour. The mother in the example of the boiling kettle knows that she has to prevent her baby reaching the kettle whenever the problem recurs. After a time he gets the message that, try as he might, the kettle is forbidden.

The way you respond should be easily understood by the child. Trying to prevent an autistic child from breaking a window by talking to him has no effect. Shouting at him may put him off at first, but he will become accustomed to that after a time. If you become angry after the window is broken, and show it very obviously, this may have the opposite effect to that which you intended. A young autistic child who does not understand the implications of the signs of rage may feel that an angry parent is an interesting and exciting event, and he will therefore be encouraged rather than deterred. This is particularly likely to happen if he is left alone when quiet, but becomes the centre of attention when he creates a disturbance. As with the baby and the kettle, it is more effective to take action to hold him and remove him before the window is broken. This has the advantage that it can be turned into a cuddle, or a tickling game, or whatever you know the child enjoys. Sometimes parents give up trying because they find that their child does not respond to their efforts to control his behaviour. This is usually because they try methods which they expect to work with a normal child, but which are meaningless to an autistic child. In this situation the parents have to be encouraged to observe as carefully as they can in order to find their own child's likes and dislikes, and then to work out a programme which will be effective in practice.

Certain kinds of behaviour cannot be anticipated or prevented. A good example is a sudden outburst of screaming for no obvious reason. Then the best method is to ignore the child, and only to attend to him when he stops doing the thing you wish to prevent. In this case, you are rewarding him through your interest and attention, a reward which he receives only when he is not indulging in the undesirable behaviour.

It is an important principle that if you want to improve a child's general behaviour you should help him find positive, constructive things to do. It is no good stopping him spending his time hitting his head against a wall, if the only alternative is to sit in a chair with no occupation at all. In these circumstances the head banging is likely to start up again.

If you sometimes prevent a problem and at other times overlook it, this seems to have a worse effect than taking no action at all. This is one example of the general finding that an inconsistent approach creates even more difficulties than over-strictness or over-permissiveness. However, consistency is difficult to achieve, particularly for a busy mother with more than one child needing her attention. For this reason it is best to decide to take a firm stand on the most important behaviour problems, but to leave the ones which are not particularly inconvenient. This compromise results in a reasonably relaxed atmosphere, but also allows the child to learn that there are limits beyond which he may not go.

The best teaching techniques in the world are no use unless they are used by someone who really loves the child concerned and has his best interests at heart. Success depends upon knowing the child, understanding his handicaps, being aware of his likes and dislikes, and being able to guess what he intends to do before he starts to do it. These insights are almost impossible to achieve in the absence of any positive feeling for the child.

i *Screaming and temper tantrums*

(The suggestions in this section apply to fits of screaming and temper tantrums which occur as part of a pattern of disturbed behaviour. They are not appropriate for screaming brought on by physical illness, or pain, or some other understandable reason. In these situations the cause has to be found and dealt with. It is not always possible to distinguish the reasons for tantrums, but parents have to rely on their experience of their own child and make the best guess they can.)

Young autistic children often have tantrums because they have no words with which to ask for the things they want. They may scream in order to obtain sweets, cakes or ice-creams, or for some oddment which interests them at the time, or because a routine has been disturbed. Parents, being only human, tend to deal with the situation by giving the child something to soothe and quieten him because they know from bitter experience that the screams can go on for hours. Unfortunately, the child, being only human too, soon 'learns' that the quickest way of getting anything he wants is to scream and shout and stamp and kick – in short to have a first-class temper tantrum. He does not work this out in words, but he learns through his own and his parents' actions.

The way to prevent, rather than to encourage, tantrums is to make sure that the child is never given the things he wants while he is actually showing this behaviour. This requires courage and determination because the policy must be put into practice in public, as well as at home. If a child has a tantrum in the street or in a shop, the only solution may be to remove him from the scene as rapidly as possible.

When at home, the child should be ignored while he is screaming. It may be possible to put him in another room away from the rest of the family, but only if he can come to no harm and do no damage while by himself. The moment the tantrum stops he should be given lots of attention and praise, and some other suitable reward such as a rough and tumble game, listening to a favourite record, holding some favourite object, or a small helping of food or drink.

Most parents who have been faced with daily temper tantrums have in desperation tried to stop the screams by slapping the child. This may have a shock effect the first few times, but if repeated too often the child ceases to take any notice and continues to scream. It is better to reserve this way of reacting for the rare emergency occasion, when something has to be done in a hurry. The method of ignoring the screams and then rewarding the child when he is quiet may take time to work (and requires iron nerves plus deaf ears) but it is the most successful in the end. Both elements are necessary. Ignoring is no use without the eventual reward, and vice versa.

Later on, when the child begins to understand and use words to some extent, he will probably respond to a firm voice and manner when a temper tantrum threatens. He is more likely to be amenable to these 'normal' methods of control if he was treated sensibly and consistently in his earlier years.

Screaming may be due to fear and distress produced by something that is in reality quite harmless. If this goes on for long, the child may lose all control and behave in exactly the same way as in a temper tantrum. It is therefore important to stop the reaction as quickly as possible. When the cause is known, the child can be removed from the fear-provoking situation and comforted. If, as often happens, he refuses all comfort, then the same tactics as for temper tantrums have to be used. The causes of the fear must be tackled, and some suggestions for this will be given further on. It may be impossible to discover the reasons for temper tantrums or for extremes of panic, which in any case are hard to tell apart. In a young child they may be a reaction to the chaos of his life which every now and again becomes unbearable. Careful planning can help to avoid these occasions (see the section on enlarging social experience, below). One special situation which disturbs many young autistic children is waking up from a sleep taken in the daytime. (Many normal people also find this an unpleasant experience.) They often go through a period in which they begin screaming almost as soon as they open their eyes, and cuddling and comforting have no effect. This is commonest around one to two years of age when they are still having a regular daytime nap. Some mothers have found that they can prevent the problem by arranging the timetable so that the child wakes while being pushed along in his pram. The movement seems to be soothing and reassuring. Giving a bottle of fruit juice, singing a nursery rhyme or playing a favourite record immediately on waking may also be effective in preventing the distress.

ii *Destructiveness*

This is a serious problem for many parents. Autistic children cannot play constructively, so they often occupy themselves by examining the simple properties of the things around them. They soon learn that paper (including books and wallpaper) tears, and that many hard things make a noise when hurled to the floor, and an even more satisfying noise when they break. One small boy developed an unerring aim with his toy bricks, and shattered all the light bulbs in his house. At a later stage, the children develop enough to want to fit one object inside another. They often do not comprehend that large into small won't go, so they break and tear to achieve their aim, perhaps having a temper tantrum from frustration at the same time. The products of excretion are easily available, and smearing the walls is added to the rest of the damage. Those autistic children who are too handicapped to be destructive are less trouble, but need even more help than those who do explore the world in these inconvenient ways.

All children need to go through a period of messy play, and some compromise is necessary. Sand, water and mud are less trouble in the garden. If possible, an area especially for the child can be fenced off from the rest. This will also preserve the flowers and vegetables which otherwise tend to suffer the same fate as indoor possessions. In the winter or if there is no garden at all, it is worth considering arranging things so that the child has one room in which to make a mess. A tray of sand and some water can be provided. Large, strong, simple objects that are pleasant to feel and to move around are useful at this stage. A blackboard to scribble on may be used later on.

The rest of the house should be out of bounds except under strict supervision. Night-time may be a special problem. The child's bedroom should be safe for him and easily cleaned. If he tears his wallpaper one night when you are asleep, there is not a lot of point in replacing it until this stage is passed. It is better to use a washable paint which cannot be torn away.

The real solution, in the end, is to help the child to become interested in more constructive activities. This takes time, because the child has to reach the stage of development at which he can be helped. In the meantime, the only thing to do is to supervise the child carefully, and take the same kind of precautions as those necessary with a very active toddler.

A reasonable amount of give and take is necessary. The children must learn that they cannot spoil other people's possessions, but they must also have possessions of their own. It is useful to teach a simple formula to indicate ownership such as 'That belongs to Daddy', 'That belongs to Mummy'. Eventually the child will realise that he must not touch the objects which are labelled in this way. If he can talk he can also be taught an appropriate phrase to indicate the things which belong to him.

iii *Socially embarrassing behaviour*

Young normal children inevitably cause acute embarrassment to their parents in public from time to time, providing many funny stories to be laughed at in retrospect. Autistic children do similar things, but they do them more often, they go on doing them for much longer, and they do them with a total lack of inhibitions.

In the early stages, anticipation is essential, to avoid incidents in which the child knocks down a huge display of tins in a supermarket, or grabs bars of chocolate from the shop counter. The children have no idea of psychological barriers and will wander behind counters and into the back premises of shops quite unconcerned. Some of them run away at any opportunity, pursuing a straight course at considerable speed, heedless of all obstacles. Another adult to accompany the mother on shopping expeditions is a help. If this cannot be arranged, walking reins are useful for the toddler. Many mothers have had to keep their child firmly strapped in the push chair while near any 'danger zones'.

The problem with these restraints is that most autistic children soon learn how to undo them or wriggle out of them. More active teaching is therefore necessary. The child should be watched, and always held firmly as soon as any difficult behaviour begins. At the same time, he should be told 'No' in a firm clear voice. He will begin to realise that 'No' is a strict prohibition and eventually the word will suffice. 'Don't touch' is another phrase which can be taught, by using it whenever you pull your child's hand away from something he must not handle. Autistic children learn these things more slowly than normal children. The period before they have learnt is bound to be difficult and wearing for the parents. They will be tempted to give up and perhaps avoid going out with the child at all, doing the shopping at inconvenient times when they can do it alone. This is a most unsatisfactory solution, because the child loses the opportunity of eventually learning reasonable behaviour.

Fortunately, older autistic children are easier in this respect, but other problems arise with the child who can talk. The children's habit of echoing words and phrases they have heard in the past can lead to unfortunate consequences. Parents have to be especially careful of the things they say in front of their child if they do not want them repeated in an exact copy of their accents and tone of voice. Swear words are particularly easy to learn because the emphasis and intensity usually accompanying them catch the attention of even a withdrawn child. Naive remarks about other people, made in a loud voice, have to be discouraged firmly. Children who can talk enough to make such remarks usually have fairly good comprehension of simple ideas. They will eventually learn that they must never talk about people's appearances, clothes or manners, if they are told many times over, using the same simple words each time. They will not understand the reason for the rule, nor will they be able to generalise to other situations, but the more advanced children may begin to realise that thoughtless remarks can make other people unhappy.

The older child's lack of appreciation of social taboos often leads to problems, especially in those children who appear normal upon superficial observation. Removing clothes or passing urine in public may be done in all innocence by an adolescent or young adult. Parents and teachers have to lay down a series of rules in an attempt to forestall or prevent a repetition of such incidents. The trouble is that no one can think of everything that might happen, and life seems too short to teach the correct response in every imaginable situation (let alone the unimaginable ones that seem to crop up as often). One can only do what one can and hope for the best. Once a rule is learnt, an autistic child tends to keep it under all circumstances. This leads to problems too, as with the child who learnt that one must always use the lavatory, and then suffered intense discomfort on a long drive in the countryside because he could not be persuaded to break the rule in this special situation.

It is important to remember to show pleasure and appreciation when an outing has passed without a mishap.

iv. *Resistance to change*

This particular problem ranks high on the list of symptoms which cause parents the most worry and despair. If not handled properly, a child's insistence on routine can come to dominate the life of the whole family. The parents of one child were unable to invite any guests for a meal because he always screamed violently if the seating arrangements for dining were changed in any way.

The behaviour is the child's pathetic attempt to introduce order into his chaotic world, and this has to be remembered when working out the best way of managing the problem. It is necessary to arrange the child's life so that it has order and pattern. He needs to know what will happen next so that he feels comfortable and secure. Change should be introduced only after preparation. When he is young, it is reasonable for him to have his own chair and his own cup, saucer and plate and place at the table, and his special toy to take to bed.

However, a firm line needs to be drawn, when the resistance to change reaches the point where it interferes with the life of the rest of the family, and also prevents the child himself from moving forward to more constructive activities. It is possible to deal with the problem by consistently refusing to allow the child to continue with his more inconvenient routines. One small girl insisted on

holding a tiny piece of photographic negative in the palm
of her hand. Whenever the negative became damp, which
inevitably happened sooner or later, she screamed until
a new dry piece was provided. This was finally solved
by ceasing to provide any more pieces. Prolonged temper
tantrums resulted but eventually the whole business was
forgotten.

Witmer, writing in 1919, described a more difficult
problem. In this case, the little boy, Don, refused to part
with a card which he held in his hand. If this were removed,
he immediately scratched his face quite badly with his
fingernails. Witmer arranged for a nurse to stay with the
child, holding his hands away from his face, gently but
firmly. The child screamed ferociously, and the nurse
remained kind, patient but immovable. She stayed with
him for several hours, releasing his hands from time to
time, but holding him again if his fingers went to his face.
Finally he could be left without the card and without harm-
ing himself. There were other problems to follow, but the
interesting point is that each was solved considerably more
easily than this first one.

Another complication arises if the child is able to find
his special objects for himself. A boy who liked tin lids
(which he bent into special shapes) and a girl who liked
detergent packets were adept at finding these in cupboards,
workshops, dustbins or other people's houses. In this case
the children have to be supervised closely until they
realise that this activity is forbidden.

Insistence on special routines can be managed in a similar
way, by refusing to fit into the child's rigid scheme. If
temper tantrums result these can be coped with in the way
suggested previously.

Parents worry a great deal as to the effect of preventing
a child from carrying out his routines or depriving him of
his collections. They wonder if this will produce some kind
of emotional damage. They can be reassured that there is

no evidence that this will occur. In fact, most parents who have had the courage to stand firm have found that once the problem has been overcome the child's behaviour and their relationship with him tend to improve. He learns that his parents are strong confident people, and also that giving up a routine does not make the world fall to pieces. He has been helped to take a small step forward and all the family gain from the experience.

A more reasonable objection is that when one routine is given up, another comes along to take its place. This is to some extent true, because the children's handicaps make them liable to this kind of behaviour. However, if one problem is overcome successfully, those that follow are easier to manage. In theory it should be possible to remove each difficulty over objects or routines as it occurs. In practice, most parents find that a compromise works well. Some of these habits comfort the child but have no adverse effect on anyone else, and these can be left alone. For example, no problem arises if a child likes to carry a smooth pebble in his pocket, as long as he does not have a tantrum if he loses it, or holds it in his hand so much that it interferes with other activities. A little girl wanted to take a large dustpan with her wherever she went. She gradually accepted the idea that the dustpan could be 'played with' at home but not in public. When she went out she would put it on a special shelf in her toy cupboard, saying 'All ready for come-back'. This formula reassured her and she would go out happily, minus the dustpan.

Once parents have made up their minds to discourage inconvenient habits, it is helpful to tackle a new one that might be troublesome as soon as it appears. The task is easier in the early stages than it is once the routine is well established. A number of mothers take deliberate steps to vary household routines just a little every day so that the children become used to the idea of a certain amount of change. This may seem to contradict my earlier suggestion that autistic children need order in their lives. As usual, what one is aiming for is a workable compromise between too much rigidity on the one hand and too little structure on the other, and in the end each family has to make its own decisions depending upon its special needs.

v *Problems with eating*

At least two different factors may be involved in feeding problems and food fads.

Firstly, some autistic children have trouble with controlling the movements of the muscles involved with chewing. They are difficult to wean because they do not know how to cope with lumpy food. (Children born both partially deaf and partially blind reject lumpy food even more often than autistic children.) Food that needs chewing has to be introduced slowly, so that the child can practise without being frightened by lumps that are too big or hard for him to manage. One mother found that she had to teach her autistic son to chew by moving his lower jaw with her hands to give him an idea of the movements required.

Speech therapists have developed a series of exercises, involving blowing bubbles, blowing pieces of cotton wool, and retrieving sweet food placed on the lips outside the mouth by using the tip of the tongue. These are designed for any child who has trouble in co-ordinating his tongue and mouth movements, and can be found in some books written for parents with handicapped children. (For example, in *Teaching the retarded child to talk* by Julia S. Molloy – see book list at end.)

The second major reason for feeding problems arises from the children's resistance to change, and their tendency to cling to special routines. All autistic children are more suspicious of new foods than even young normal children. The best way to manage food fads in a normal child is to provide a good mixed diet, and adopt an attitude of casual indifference to how much is eaten, since a normal child can be trusted not to starve. Minor eating problems in autistic children can be dealt with in the same way. If the child takes in adequate quantities of protein, fat, carbohydrate, vitamins and fluid overall, it does not matter if for example he refuses certain kinds of food, or eats only one meal a day. In this situation, there is no need for a mother to cook special food for the autistic child – perhaps because the rest of the family likes carrots and the autistic child never touches them. He can go without occasionally without coming to any harm, and he is more likely to come round to trying something new if he is hungry and knows he will get nothing else.

A useful technique with a child who has some understanding and use of words is to introduce a new food or drink with reference to something similar which goes down well. A girl of eight refused to consider a cup of drinking chocolate, until she was told it was 'chocolate-coffee'. She tasted it and liked it at once.

If a feeding problem starts in a child who has previously eaten reasonably well the parents should make sure that the child does not have some physical illness such as a fever which has made him lose his appetite. If there is any doubt a doctor's advice should be sought. Once it is clear that there is no physical cause which should be treated, the same principles of management apply to this problem as to other difficulties that arise. The child should not be 'rewarded' for refusing food by having constant anxious attention paid to him at every meal time. He should not be pressed to eat at all times of the day, or given unsuitable foods (such as sweets or cakes) just to make sure he eats something. He should be given food at meal times only, and in rather small quantities so that every mouthful is needed because he is hungry. Uneaten food should be removed without comment, and a good long empty gap left until the next meal.

Sometimes problems with food assume major proportions. A number of autistic children go through phases in which their diet is restricted to, for example, hamburgers, or lettuce and bananas. A very few cases have been reported in which the child will eat nothing at all. It almost seems as if the child does not connect up the feeling of inner emptiness with the idea of eating food. The problem may disappear of its own accord after a few days, but if the child persists in eating a severely limited diet, then medical advice is needed. One doctor who specialises in paediatrics admits children with this problem into hospital. There they are gradually introduced to new foods by mixing them in with the one or two things they will eat, as a 'camouflage'. The children are allowed nothing at all between meals, and the food is removed if they refuse to eat. Their physical health can be closely supervised during this period. All of the children treated came to like the new foods and eventually ate a normal diet. The scheme was most successful if mothers were admitted at the same time, and taught how to manage meal times at home, to avoid a relapse. The programme of care also included playtimes and perceptual training, once the child had begun to accept a more reasonable range of food.

Fortunately, extreme feeding problems are rather rare. Minor ones are more common. They are inconvenient but not likely to result in any harm to the child, and can be managed with common sense and confidence.

Children who eat poorly at home may develop hearty appetites when they begin school, helped by the example of the other children and the sensible attitude of the staff.

vi *Special fears*

Some autistic children are always tense and fearful, and almost all of them develop fears of harmless things at some

time or other. It is usually difficult to know the origin of
the fears, but sometimes it is possible to trace them back
to their beginnings. One little girl had a pair of new shoes
which were uncomfortable because they rubbed her heels.
From then on she screamed and refused to walk if shoes
were put on her feet. A small boy put his finger into a bath
of water which was a little too hot, and could not be persuaded to enter the bath for years after that, although he
was quite happy to sit in the large kitchen sink.

Normal children have similar experiences which may
alarm them when they are small, but they can communicate
their fears to their parents and accept verbal reassurance
and explanation. Autistic children have no way of asking
for help, and uncomfortable events tend to confirm their
fears of the world and their dislike of any change.

The behaviour which was first caused by fear may continue as a routine habit long after the fear has gone. In this
case it can be dealt with in the same way as other routines.
Before this stage is reached the problem is more difficult to
solve because the child's terror is so obvious, and parents
feel acute distress if they try to force the child into situations
in which he is fearful.

Sometimes it is possible to change the child's behaviour
by gradual exposure to the frightening situation. For
example, the little girl who would not wear shoes was
helped in the following way. At the time she loved to eat
boiled eggs. When she had her egg for tea, a pair of slippers
in her favourite colour was placed beside her, while she was
eating, and taken away before she had finished. Without
the egg the slippers produced screams, but with the egg
they were accepted calmly. The time with the slippers was
lengthened, and then the stage was reached when they
could be put on her feet while she was eating. The time with
slippers on was again lengthened until she cheerfully
wore them all through tea. After this, her outdoor shoes
were tried, and these produced no fearful reaction. She

wore them without any fuss, and from then on they were put on in the morning in the usual way. The fear never recurred, and buying new shoes is now looked forward to as a pleasant occasion.

It is not always possible to carry out this kind of plan. Chocolate sweets were tried for the boy who was afraid of the bath tub, but the fear was too strong to be soothed by the sweets. It is interesting that this problem was eventually overcome in a different way. A new *au-pair* girl who was good with children popped him into a bath during the daytime, on the first day of her stay with the family, unaware of his fear. His astonished mother heard happy giggles and splashes and found her child enjoying his first bath in years as if he had one every day. The same *au-pair* girl, encouraged by her success, persuaded the same child to use the adult lavatory, of which he had previously been afraid. In this case, it seems that the child was helped by the different expectations of the *au-pair* girl. She was not anticipating fear whereas his parents had grown accustomed to it. They also learnt from the experience, and were much more confident (and successful) in dealing with other similar problems which occurred after this incident. Hair-washing, and hair and nail-cutting is disliked by all young children but may cause intense fear and furious resistance in an autistic child. Since these things have to be done, parents must persist as calmly as they can, and never give up once they have started, even if one person has to hold the child while the other washes or trims. Eventually the problem eases and passes away, especially if the child becomes interested in his appearance. Visits to a hairdresser who is good with children should be started as early as possible so that this becomes an accepted routine.

It usually happens that once the child is persuaded to face the things that frighten him his fears dissolve away. An autistic girl refused to do more than stand in the water at the seaside and screamed if anyone tried to hold her with her feet off the bottom. One day she suddenly found that she was able to float with her special arm bands and swimming ring, and from that moment she was utterly without fear of the sea (although this had its inconvenient side too).

Some families have dealt with their child's fear of dogs by buying a puppy. This usually works well although it is wise to choose a dog from a reputable breeder and of a type that is likely to be placid and good with children when it grows up. It is also sensible to prepare the child by showing him pictures of dogs, and toy models of dogs in advance.

It should be remembered that autistic children can develop certain fears because of their sensitivity to loud noises and bright lights. This may lie behind fears of, for example, aeroplanes, trains, motor bikes, barking dogs and photographers' flash lights. They seem to find these stimuli quite painful, and are not making a fuss about nothing. Calm reassurance and distraction of the child's attention may help. Fortunately the sensitivity becomes less troublesome as time goes on. Sympathy for the child should not prevent one from being fairly firm about riding in trains or aeroplanes if these journeys are necessary. Once inside, most of the children find the noise level tolerable, and in any case they nearly all enjoy the movement, so that fear gives place to pleasure.

The children tend to be confused if they wake in the night. This is also true of normal children and adults if they wake suddenly from a deep sleep, but the problem seems more severe and longer lasting in autistic children. They may appear particularly fearful and distressed in these circumstances, and are hard to comfort because they resist being touched or cuddled. They may be soothed by a reassuring manner, a calm and gentle tone of voice, and perhaps hearing a favourite song or nursery rhyme.

Each fear has to be considered, and a decision made whether to deal with it by slowly increasing exposure linked with something that is enjoyed, or by showing the child at once that there is nothing to be frightened of, or else by allowing the child to avoid the situation until he can be helped to overcome it at a later stage.

The key to the problem is confidence. If the parents feel confident in what they are doing, then the child will respond and the difficulties will be resolved. Once this has happened, of course, it is easier to have confidence in one's ability to solve the next problem. It is taking the first step which is so hard. Experienced teachers have a natural advantage over parents in these matters, because they have been through similar situations many times before, and no longer feel worried and unsure of themselves. It often happens, therefore, that a seemingly insoluble problem dissolves away when the child starts to attend school.

vii *Lack of fear of real dangers*

This is the opposite side of the picture to the children's special fears, but can be equally worrying. Many parents remember how their child walked into the water, fully clothed, on his first visit to the seaside. The children who like climbing tend to have at least one heart-stopping feat to their credit, such as walking along a narrow ledge on the roof or hanging out of the window practically by their toes. They are usually so sure-footed that no harm results, but there have been a few instances in which children have been injured or even killed because they were oblivious of real danger.

Parents have to be aware of this. They can teach the rules for crossing the road, avoiding fires, electricity and gas, and warn the children of other common dangers, but even the brightest autistic child will learn these by rote, and may not apply them to a new situation. It may be necessary to put bars on a young child's window, and to keep various doors in the house locked. The keys should be kept in a place which cannot be reached by a child because the children may have no difficulty in learning how to undo locks. All possible sources of danger both inside and outside the house have to be considered and proper precautions organised. As with every other problem, the worst time is between two and five years of age. The children do tend to become more aware of danger as they grow older – at least they are more willing to obey the rules.

viii *Odd movements and grimaces*

The children's tendency to show odd movements is a problem for two main reasons. Firstly they look peculiar and draw undesirable attention in public. Secondly, the children seem to derive some satisfaction or stimulation from their movements and grimaces, and may keep them up for hours, rather than engage in any constructive activity.

If an adult works with a child and engages him in some occupation, the odd movements hardly occur at all. They are rarely seen in a properly run school which provides a structured environment and a detailed timetable for the whole day. They are at their worst when the child has nothing to do. Therefore one of the most useful ways of dealing with this behaviour is to occupy the child as fully as possible.

The movements have to be discouraged when out shopping, on outings or anywhere in public. Gently holding the child's hands when he twists and turns them gradually gives him the idea that this behaviour is not acceptable. The action can be linked with a word or a phrase so that eventually this alone will remind him.

ix *Self-destructiveness*

This is yet another problem that autistic children share with children who are born both deaf and blind. Like the odd movements it occurs more often if the children are unoccupied. It is most obvious in children who live in large understaffed institutions, and who have to be left to their own devices for most of the time. The major part of the solution is therefore the organising of the child's day to give him plenty to do.

Psychologists who are specially interested in methods of behaviour modification describe how children in institutions often receive attention from the staff only when they begin to harm themselves. The staff may run to comfort them, or to scold them, when this happens, but otherwise the children may be ignored. It is easy to see how this will make the self-injury occur more often than ever, although it started originally because the child was bored and unoccupied. Some workers have stopped children seriously injuring themselves by punishing this behaviour, and giving the child praise and attention only when he is not biting, scratching or head-banging. These methods have had to be used because the self-injury had gone on so long and had assumed such alarming proportions. The individual attention and stimulation of family life is the best way of preventing this distressing behaviour.

Even when they are living at home the children do sometimes bite, or hurt themselves in other ways. This may happen because of some minor frustration, or when the child becomes upset and confused through his inability to understand. (This is bound to happen from time to time even in the best possible environment.) The children often bite the backs of their wrists and hands, and look very tense and angry when they do this. The best way to deal with this situation is to sort out the confusion (perhaps a misunderstanding of verbal instructions) or to take some action concerning the reason for the frustration, depending on its cause.

Self-injury in a well-cared-for child may also occur during a temporary period of unhappiness. The parents of one little girl of eight years old were away from home for a week, leaving her with someone whom she knew and liked. While they were away she tended to pick at sore places and even prick her fingers with an open safety pin. She needed a lot of extra care and comforting during this time, especially since she could not use words to express her feelings nor understand enough to know when her parents were due to return. It may require much patience and detailed knowedge of the child to discover the source of the unhappiness unless it is as obvious as in the case I described. The sudden occurrence of this symptom in an autistic child should be a signal for the parents to look for a cause.

x *The very withdrawn child*

So far I have described the difficult behaviour of autistic children who are active and react to their handicaps with a kind of angry determination. There are other children who respond in a different way. They are quiet and withdrawn, tending to isolate themselves from the world, rather than hitting their heads against it in rage and frustration. They may be unchildlike in their neatness and cleanliness, because they never explore their environment, and have no interest in mud, sand or water. In contrast to the active autistic child who climbs to the top shelf of the cupboard to reach forbidden objects and undoes locks in a way that Houdini would have envied, the passive children may do nothing for themselves. They give the impression that their hands lack the strength even to lift a spoon to their mouths, or to handle a toy which is placed in front of them.

This kind of child gives less practical trouble than those who are full of energy, but they tend to be far more aloof, and cause their parents deep sadness and anxiety for this reason. In some ways, also, it is easier for a mother to feel she has something positive to do, when she has to cope with an active 'naughty' child. The self-contained passive child makes most parents feel lost, helpless and worst of all, unnecessary and unwanted.

The task of the parents here is to lead the child into the world by showing him that it is not a fearful place, and that efforts produce enjoyable consequences. This involves encouraging the child, rather than restraining his behaviour, and the suggestions under the headings of 'Teaching basic skills' and 'Enlarging social experience' may be of help. The book *The Siege*, written by Clara Claiborne Park, who is a parent of a child of this kind, gives an excellent and moving description of the way in which she helped her autistic daughter, together with much detailed advice which other parents can follow.

TEACHING BASIC SKILLS

This section is not intended to persuade parents to take on the role of teachers. Some parents have had to shoulder the whole burden of the education of their autistic child by themselves, because there was no alternative, and they have sometimes succeeded remarkably well. However, it is only the rare person with no other commitments, plus a genuine flair for teaching, who can take on the task. The roles of teacher and parent are hard to combine, and the ideal solution is for the handicapped child to live at home and to attend a special school. He then gets the best of both worlds.

Nevertheless, parents teach their normal children the simple skills of everyday living, and social relationships, and they need to know how to teach their autistic children the same things. Most people manage to bring up a normal child in the light of the ideas on child-rearing which are commonly held in their particular culture. These ideas are modified by experience but are useful as a rough and ready guide. Autistic children are a different problem altogether. It seems to the bewildered parents that none of the ordinary rules and expectations apply at all. They have rather the same emotions as a sparrow faced with a cuckoo in her nest – but, like the sparrow, they have little time for philosophical speculations and have to get on with the job as best they can.

In fact the rules which psychologists have found to govern the process of learning do apply to autistic children, but as usual the application in practice has to be modified to fit in with the problems of a child who cannot talk and cannot understand language.

The first of these rules I have already mentioned in relation to managing difficult behaviour, but it is worth repeating. Children (and adults as well) are likely to learn behaviour which is 'rewarded' (meaning that the behaviour has consequences which are enjoyable for the person concerned) and are likely to refrain from behaviour which has unpleasant results.

The second rule is that new skills are learned more easily if they are broken down into very tiny simple steps, instead of being presented all at once. This is reflected in the old saying, 'You must learn to walk before you can run.' Autistic children are especially liable to be upset by failure, and making sure that the child can succeed with each small stage is a good way of avoiding this problem.

Thirdly, a child can be encouraged to try a new skill by prompting him, fairly obviously at first, then less and less as time goes on.

The fourth rule is that it is helpful to link new learning with skills which are already familiar and which give pleasure. This is particularly appropriate for autistic children whose interest is hard to rouse. A special example of this rule is the use of a well learned skill as an aid in acquiring a new idea. A child may be able to understand the meaning of 'large' and 'small' but not be able to name colours. The first step is to make sure that he is not colour blind by finding out if he can sort a mixture of different coloured buttons into single colour piles. If this can be done, the next step is to select two colours, and then make a single large square of one colour (for example red), and a series of squares of the other colour (for example green) ranging from very small up to the size of the one large red square. Then the child is shown the large red square and the smallest green square. He is told the names of the colours and taught (by rewarding if necessary) to name, or point to, red or green when told. He will learn this because he can already name 'large' and 'small' and he will take his cue from the size of the squares, ignoring the colour. The series of green squares is then shown to the child, in ascending order of size, one after the other. Each time he has to name or point to red and green. Somewhere along the line, as the squares become more and more alike in size, he will realise that it is the colour he is supposed to name and not the size. The penny may drop suddenly and the child will show a flash of understanding and intense pleasure. It is usually unnecessary to teach all colour names in this way once the first two are learnt. The rest come by pointing them out and naming them. This technique, well known to psychologists, can be adapted for learning other skills.

It is important, when considering how to teach an autistic child a new skill, to have detailed knowledge of his handicaps. This point is ignored by some of the psychologists working in the field, although others are keenly aware of its relevance. To take one example, a child may be unable to distinguish and name the letters of the alphabet correctly. One possible reason is that he has a general problem of comprehension which prevents him from understanding which aspects of a particular letter determine its name. For example, a normal child can be told that b is a complete circle attached to an up-stroke on the left, but c has no up-stroke, and is an incomplete circle. An autistic child will not understand this explanation and may name the letters according to their size alone, even though he can see the other differences. A second possible reason for the inability to distinguish two letters is that he cannot see that they are different because of his special handicaps. This is likely to occur in the case of the letters b and d, which are mirror images of each other, if the child has difficulty in distinguishing left from right.

In the first case, the method of teaching colour names described above can be successfully adapted to teaching the names of letters. In the second case, the method will be unsuccessful, and the moment of understanding as the letter sizes approach each other will not occur. Instead the child may become anxious and distressed. The problem is shown clearly when a child can learn to distinguish a and c, but not b and d. In this case it is clear that the difficulty is not due to lack of co-operation but to a problem of perception. For each particular child and for each particular learning problem, it is necessary to determine the reason for the difficulty, and then to plan one's teaching methods on the basis of this knowledge. Unfortunately, there are as yet few teachers who are experienced in the problems of autistic children, and no specialised training is available.

Autistic children tend to go through phases in which they make little or no progress, and then, suddenly, they acquire a new skill, or take a step forward in language and social development. Sometimes they appear to learn something without preliminary practice, as with the boy of nine who tied his own shoelaces one day, after his mother had tied them for him every morning up to that time. Occasionally a child will perform a new skill once only and then revert to his previous behaviour, and it may be many years before he tries again. It is realistic to expect a slow rate of progress, on a different time-scale from that of a normal child. On the other hand, it is some comfort to know that, in most autistic children, improvement (slow but perceptible) continues throughout childhood, adolescence and adult life. There is no justification for the idea that there is a definite age limit beyond which no further change can be expected.

i *General co-operation*

Life becomes easier and happier if you can teach your child to come when you call his name, to sit down with you for a while, and to accept and enjoy the physical contact that is necessary for non-verbal learning.

Parents tend to use all kinds of pet names for their children, including versions of their given names. This is fun to do, and is a demonstration of family love and solidarity, but while an autistic child is learning to know his name it is probably best to use one only that is agreed by everyone. Once he does respond to this name, there is no problem about learning the other versions.

To begin with, the child's name should always be used in connection with situations which are pleasant for him. For example, if he is the kind of child who enjoys his meals, you should call his name as you prepare to give him his food. If he can see the plate coming, and is looking forward to eating his dinner, the sound of his name will begin to have happy associations. The name should be used in other situations as well, to make sure that he does not learn that 'Johnny' means 'dinner' and nothing else. When you give him a drink, a biscuit, a sweet, or call him to get ready for a walk (showing him what is intended by holding his coat ready to put on) or while you prepare for an enjoyable activity, you can use his name to gain his attention. At first you will probably have to hold his hand and lead him towards the food, or whatever it is you are arranging, saying his name at the same time. This kind of teaching is easier to manage if two adults work together, one leading the child and the other calling his name and showing him his coat, food, drink or whatever is appropriate. In time, the name alone will be sufficient. You can then use a simple phrase like 'Johnny – dinner' or 'Johnny – walk',

'Johnny – orange juice' so that he can learn that his name is to make him look round or come, and the second word tells him what will happen.

In the early stages do not use his name when you are angry, because this could have the reverse effect of your special teaching. It is also sensible not to use his name a great deal in situations where you do not want him to respond. You should, for instance, avoid discussing him in his presence, because this allows him to fall back into the habit of hearing his name spoken but ignoring it.

I have already mentioned the necessity of teaching the meaning of 'No' and 'Don't touch' when discussing socially embarrassing behaviour. These are prohibitions, and have to be taught by combining the words with physically preventing the child from carrying out the forbidden act. Once you have stopped him, and removed the temptation, you must not show anger or continue using the sharp tone that went with the word 'No'. He has done what you wanted (even if it was because you gave him no choice) therefore he should enjoy your love and approval. There is little point in learning to do what mother says if she continues to be cross and irritable afterwards. Later on when he can talk and when he can remember, then it may be useful to disapprove of bad behaviour some time after it has occurred (if for instance, you find out about it too late to prevent it), but this can only be done when the child has reached the appropriate stage of development.

Some autistic children struggle against certain kinds of physical contact. They usually enjoy tickling and being swung round and other fairly vigorous play. This can be used to lead on to more gentle touching and cuddling. The usual pattern can be followed of associating contact with other enjoyable experiences such as the mid-morning orange-juice drink, a meal, listening to a record, or singing a nursery rhyme. It may be necessary to start with a few seconds of contact only and then gradually to increase the time. The child has to learn to accept and enjoy your touch so that you can guide him while he is learning various useful skills.

Sitting quietly on a chair has to be learnt in small stages in the same way. An autistic child can learn that he will not have his food unless he sits quietly at the meal table. Some families find every mealtime a nightmare because their handicapped child insists on eating his food in snatches while running round the room. There is not much point in keeping a young child sitting at table waiting for everyone else to finish but he should stay at least until he has finished his own meal. Later on, he has to learn to wait for others if he is to have the pleasure of eating in restaurants with the rest of the family, but this can be taught gradually.

Sitting at a table in order to play with puzzles or to draw comes as part of the process of gaining interest in the occupation. Once these activities are enjoyed by the child it is not difficult to show him that he can only have the equipment as long as he is willing to sit and play with it, and that when he becomes restless it will be put away.

I have several times mentioned using food and mealtimes as an aid to learning. This idea arouses strong opposition in some people, because they feel that this is 'training' rather than teaching, and that using basic needs as motives is not appropriate for children. The answer is that with a very young severely handicapped child who cannot understand any of the usual ways of teaching, one has to use whatever is at hand to help the child 'catch on' to what is wanted. Food is the easiest and surest thing to start with (as long as the child enjoys eating and does not have a food problem), but there are plenty of other rewards that can be used later. Going out for a walk, listening to records, hearing nursery songs, tickling and cuddling, whispering into the child's ear, playing with water, riding in a car, giving a pick-a-back ride can all be used depending on the child's special likes and dislikes. Parents soon find that even if they have to start with food, they can go on to other kinds of rewards, and eventually their approval will be sufficient, although it may not be enough when starting a new activity. Anyone with practical experience of young autistic children would agree that it is better for a child to start helping him as soon as possible, rather than to refuse to use food as a reward because of theoretical objections.

A more practical problem is that the foods most liked by children tend to be sweets and biscuits. If these are used between meals they spoil the appetite for more nutritious food, may lead to overweight, and furthermore, they are bad for the teeth. If the child likes little pieces of apple or other fruit, these problems are less serious. Conventional mealtimes can be used for teaching. If there is no choice but to use sweets, then tiny pieces of a variety that does not have to be chewed (plus good general dental care) are the best compromise. Other ways of motivating the child should be used as soon as possible.

ii Resistance to learning and negativism

Autistic children, when they are young, appear to be resistant to learning new skills. Sometimes they seem to refuse to do anything that is required of them. When a skill is learnt, a child may repeat it again and again until its performance seems meaningless, and he may resist any attempt to move on to another task. Careful observation of the situations in which the children respond with stubborn resistance to, or a withdrawal from, teaching, will begin to give some idea of the reasons for this behaviour.

Some children show more resistance than others. Usually, the more a child is able to talk and to comprehend language, the less negative behaviour he shows. Even the most stubborn child is more willing to work at some tasks than at others. The important factor seems to be how much the child understands what you want him to do. If he cannot guess from what you are saying, and has trouble imitating the things he sees you doing, it is not particularly surprising that he does the wrong thing, or does nothing at all. Depending on the personality of the child concerned, continued attempts to make him perform might lead to a temper tantrum, severe anxiety, or to withdrawal.

Although the basic problem underlying a negative attitude is a genuine lack of understanding, there is no doubt that secondary difficulties arise. Confusion is a most unpleasant emotion, and repeated failure is depressing. The children come to associate every teaching situation with these unhappy feelings, and start to react against learning almost as soon as a task is presented. In this they are no different from an otherwise normal child who has a specific difficulty with reading, and who develops emotional disturbances as a consequence of his primary handicap. Many of the children become upset if their mistakes are corrected when they have begun to learn a new skill. They may scream, bite the backs of their hands, and appear to be anxious and distressed. This in turn upsets the teacher, and an inexperienced person may be frightened to continue. The problem can be minimised by making sure that the explanations are simple. If a child makes a mistake, the steps in learning may have to be made even smaller. It helps to remain calm and confident and reassuring. If you feel the child can succeed, you must be firm, and show that he has to try, but without losing your temper. Your confidence will communicate itself to the child.

Another factor complicating the children's learning problems may have a physical cause. Some parents notice that their autistic children seem to have good days and bad days. Sometimes they are more alert, more interested in the world, and more willing to learn. At other times, perhaps even the next day, they are withdrawn, irritable, and refuse

94

to co-operate. These swings are most marked in the early years. Occasionally parents say that they notice that their child's appearance is subtly different on his bad days, his face being puffy and his eyes tired – although this may follow the crying and temper tantrums rather than preceding them. If a child sometimes co-operates well and sometimes refuses to do anything, he may not be 'trying to be awkward' – his handicaps may be harder to overcome on some days than on others, for reasons beyond his control. In any case, if someone is trying to perform at the upper limits of his skill his performance will be far more variable than it would be if he were working well within his resources. The ups and downs shown by world-class sportsmen in important matches are an example of an extreme situation, but an autistic child has to work just as hard to cope with everyday life.

Careful attention to correct methods of teaching helps to overcome the problems caused by lack of understanding. The child can be given tasks prepared in such a way that he has a chance of succeeding and when he does succeed he should be shown approval in ways that he can understand. Under these conditions so-called 'negativism' becomes much less troublesome, as long as training is not pushed beyond the child's capabilities.

There is no point in trying to teach an autistic child a new skill before the age at which one would expect success with a normal child. In fact, since most autistic children are retarded in development teaching is more likely to succeed if it is started rather later than it would be with normal children. If, after trying to teach a child, it becomes obvious that his handicaps prevent him from learning some particular task, it should be left for a while and then tried again. It requires considerable insight and judgment to decide at any particular stage if increased pressure will help a child to succeed, or if it will intensify his confusion and anxiety. There is no easy answer to this problem, and parents and teachers have to decide in the light of their knowledge of and feeling for the child, and their past experience. Some mistakes are inevitable but fortunately their effects are by no means irrevocable.

I shall now mention a few of the areas in which parents can help their children at home.

iii *Toilet training*

Some autistic children are toilet-trained at the same time as the average normal child. Others remain incontinent for several years. The same training methods can be used as with normal children, but they require patience and persistence. The best thing is not to make any fuss about the child's mistakes, but to put him on his pot or on the lavatory regularly at the times when he is most likely to use them. These are on waking after a dry night or daytime sleep, after meals and after drinks given between meals. Each child has to be observed carefully so that the time between eating or drinking, and emptying bowels or bladder can be worked out fairly accurately. He should remain on his pot or on the lavatory for a few minutes. If successful he should be given lots of praise and attention, or some other reward which he likes. If nothing happens, no comment should be made.

Some children seem to dislike or even fear the pot or toilet seat. It is worth while finding out if they feel insecure. Small pot-chairs can be bought which are stable and comfortable. An adult-size lavatory may be too high off the ground for a small child, so something to place his feet on will help. A very cold toilet seat will be enough to worry some children.

Even with patience and persistence, it may be a long time before an autistic child can go without nappies. People who write on child care advise parents that they should change a wet or soiled nappy as soon as possible, so that the child

does not become used to being wet, and therefore unconcerned about the discomfort.

iv *Self-care*

This includes dressing, using knife, fork and spoon,
washing, brushing and combing hair, cleaning teeth and all
the other necessities of daily living. Normal children,
encouraged by their parents, try to imitate these activities
which they see performed by other members of the family.
When they are strong enough and well co-ordinated enough
they begin to co-operate in the care given by their mothers,
and soon want to take over these functions for themselves.
They want to try feeding themselves and dressing themselves
even if they make a mess in the process. Autistic children,
on the other hand, may go through a phase, around one or
two years of age, of actively resisting attempts to wash and
dress them. Every item of daily care may precipitate a
tantrum at this stage. Later on they tend to accept all
these attentions passively, like little dolls rather than children.

Teaching them to care for themselves involves a method
which can be applied in many different situations. The
children cannot learn by being *told* how, nor by being *shown*
how, but they can learn by *feeling* how to do things. If a
child's limbs and fingers are held and moved through the
pattern of movements necessary for a particular skill he will
eventually realise what is required of him. If you want
him to do up his buttons, you should choose a garment with
large buttons and easy buttonholes on the front, within
reach of his fingers. You stand behind him and hold his
hands firmly but not too tightly so that you can put them
through the movements necessary for fastening the buttons.
You can encourage him while you do this if he likes to
hear you speak, but if he is the kind of child who becomes
worried and upset by talking while he is involved in a new

task, it is best to keep silent. You can hug and praise him when the buttons are done up. One button is probably enough to start with.

At first his fingers will feel limp, and you will find that you are doing all the work. This may last for weeks, but eventually you will begin to feel some tension in his hands. Little by little he will follow your movements until in the end he is doing the job himself. He will probably continue to need the touch of your hand on his arm to encourage him for some time, but in the end you can remove even this support, and doing up his own buttons will become second nature to him.

Most of the other elementary skills of self-care can be tackled in the same way as long as they are broken down into simple steps. As each one is learnt, the next one becomes easier to teach. Dressing is rather a special problem because it involves putting things on the right way out and the right way round. If you consider all the operations involved in putting on a pullover with the seams inside and the V-neck in front, you can see that it is a most complicated activity. Autistic children who are confused about up-down, back-front and right-left will learn to put their clothes on, but will need extra help for a long time if the result is to be acceptable. To start with, it will be necessary to place the clothes in front of the child so that they will end up in the correct position, and give a guiding hand when necessary. Later on, helpful labels which should go inside and at the back can be pointed out to the child, but success requires years of practice.

Brushing and combing hair involves using a mirror for a presentable result. Problems of right-left orientation therefore complicate this skill also, and complete success depends on practice plus increasing maturity.

The children should be encouraged to feed themselves even if they are messy eaters. They may have to use a spoon and fork for a long time, but eventually they should be able to graduate to a knife and fork. Some of them find problems in co-ordinating a knife and fork for cutting food (as in the English method of eating) and may prefer the American style of eating pre-cut food with a fork alone.

One special problem is that autistic children do not have much conception of a finished result. They do not put the final touches to dressing, such as tucking shirt inside trousers, or pulling up the socks neatly. Hair tends to be brushed the requisite number of times without regard to the actual style in which it is supposed to be worn, and face and hands may be washed with vigour, but without removing streaks of dirt on areas left untouched by the operation. They are often unaware of which clothes are suitable for the prevailing weather, and will put on thick underclothes in the summer, or light cotton dresses in the winter. Supervision and tactful assistance (without nagging) have to be available, and are usually necessary even for adolescents and adults.

An interest in clothes and general appearance is a good thing to encourage. It is worth while taking extra trouble to dress a girl, or a boy for that matter, so that he or she looks as neat and attractive as possible. This is a help towards being accepted socially, and also gives plenty of opportunity for people to make nice remarks to the child. As they grow older the children begin to realise that all this is pleasant and they learn to be concerned about their clothes and enjoy expeditions to buy new ones. This is a happy contrast to the early years in which many autistic children bitterly resent any attempt to try on garments in shops.

v *Helping in the home*

Handicapped children are dependent for so long and need so much special care that they tend to become completely passive members of their families. It is better for them if they have some positive role to play, however limited this may be. Autistic children, once they have become reasonably co-operative and willing to learn, can be taught many simple tasks. Laying the table with cutlery is a good one to begin with, since there is nothing to break if dropped. It has the special advantage that it involves remembering and naming each person in the family who has a place at table. Each one has the same implements, and this gives the opportunity of learning to use and understand the words 'knife', 'fork' and 'spoon'. Many children will have difficulty in knowing on which side to place the knives and forks, but this is all good practice in learning left from right. The process is begun by putting things in the child's hands, taking him to the table and guiding his hand to lay the places. All the family should show their appreciation of his help.

Clearing the table, putting out the milk bottles, carrying a small shopping bag, pushing a trolley in a supermarket, wheeling a small wheelbarrow in the garden can all be taught if you have enough patience. Jobs which are quick to perform and finish are best to start with. It is more difficult to persuade the children to persist at an endless task like clearing leaves from the garden lawn. They cannot understand the purpose and soon wander away. When they are older they may become better at these rather boring occupations.

If a task involves a sequence of operations, young autistic children often forget the steps involved. One little girl of seven was helping in the garden by taking a basket full of weeds to the compost heap. She set off down the long garden path, then after a few yards she stopped and looked puzzled. Her father repeated the instructions, her face cleared and she set off again, only to stop once more. She finally reached the destination and disposed of the weeds, but had to have the separate instructions repeated four times altogether. After a while she had the whole task clear in her mind and could carry it out unaided. The children need much attention to prevent them from losing interest because they cannot carry in their minds all the steps involved in a job.

vi *Physical activities*

Since autistic children have little capacity for creative play, it is especially useful to encourage physical activities which are enjoyable without the need for imagination.

Swings and slides and rocking horses are usually popular. The more anxious autistic children may refuse to try them, but it is worth while persevering to overcome the fear because of the pleasure to be found in these activities. If the child is taken to the local park he must be watched carefully at first, because he may run straight into a swing being used by another child without being aware of the danger. He will also have to learn to take his turn. This is a valuable lesson but there may be many temper tantrums and painful scenes while it is being learnt. Once a child realises that this kind of behaviour means a swift exit from the playground, he will begin to accept the waiting with better grace.

Riding a tricycle can be taught with the help of two adults One should guide the child's feet round the pedals and the other should hold his hands on the handlebars. When he experiences the necessary movements he will begin to pedal for himself. Riding a two-wheeled cycle is much more difficult since it involves balance as well as muscular effort. Some autistic children learn this with surprising ease but some never succeed. It sometimes happens that a child is given a bicycle at seven or eight years of age, but he does not learn to ride and soon loses interest. The bicycle is put away and forgotten until, several years later, the child's parents are amazed to see him pedalling it along the garden path as if he had been able to ride all his life.

ENLARGING SOCIAL EXPERIENCE

Some people have questioned whether it is desirable to

modify the behaviour of autistic children and to teach them things the purpose of which they cannot understand. These people have, on the whole, worked on the theory that if the children are in a loving environment they will in time become normal. It is sad that experience has shown that this does not happen. The children who make most progress are those who are given an opportunity to learn in an ordered, structured environment.

One of the reasons for this is that the basic learning of reasonable behaviour and the simple skills of living opens the way to a wider range of social experience which is denied to the child who is too difficult to be taken out.

i *Exploring the world*

The children can make the most of social experience when they reach the stage at which the world makes some sense to them – when they can predict at least a few simple consequences of the things that happen. Parents and teachers have to help autistic children build up a picture of the world brick by brick. The process is started by encouraging the children to explore the world to the best of their ability. Many of them show their immaturity in the way they examine themselves, other people and objects. At the age of four or five years an autistic child may still regard his own hand emerging from a sleeve as if he had not seen it before. He may bend down to look at things backwards through his legs, or try the effect of pulling the corners of his eyelids, and filling his eyes with tears, apparently to see whether the world appears different that way. This is strongly reminiscent of the description given by the psychologist Piaget of the normal very young child who regarded her own feet from different viewpoints, at the time when she was still too immature to realise that objects remain the same even though their appearance changes depending on the angle from which they are seen. Games and songs involving touching and tickling ('This little piggy', 'Round and round the garden') are useful because they teach the child about his own body as well as making him laugh.

There are surprising gaps in the world of an autistic child. He may not realise that his own house is a separate entity from the other houses in the row. It is a good idea to point out to him the windows and the door, and the boundaries which separate the house and garden from the others next door. Drawing and naming afterwards is also useful.

When the child is beginning to take some interest in the world, you can help by making sure that he knows what is going on and why things happen. For example, if the family car has to be repaired, you can tell him in simple words that the car has gone away, and the man in the garage will mend it. If there are many visible signs, such as a dented bumper, he can look at that before and after the repair. If he goes to the garage with you he can say 'Bye bye, car, see you another day' or whatever phrase you know he will understand.

Some children are interested in road works and building operations. If these are going on in the neighbourhood, they can be included in the daily walk so that progress can be seen and commented upon. It is always safest to assume that an autistic child does not understand the reason for any event in his environment, unless you can explain it to him in as simple a way as possible, and continue to repeat the explanation at every opportunity.

ii *Language and communication*

Success in teaching an autistic child to communicate depends to a great extent on his in-built potential, which in turn depends upon the severity of his handicaps. Given this inherent limitation, however, a great deal can be done to help a child to use his given potential to the full.

Psychologists who are interested in the processes of learning have given much attention to the problem of teaching autistic children to speak and to use language. They have developed methods of building speech from the simplest sounds that the child can make, by rewarding each tiny step forward. The work done by these psychologists on managing behaviour problems, discussed earlier, has been successful. There is more doubt about the eventual effects of teaching language in the same way. Many children who were previously mute do learn to say words and even phrases, but so far no strong evidence has been produced to show that their ability to use language in a mature and flexible fashion improves at the same time. It is to be hoped that future work will clarify this whole problem.

As far as parents are concerned, unless they have special training, they cannot put these detailed techniques into practice at home. They can, however, learn one or two useful lessons from the psychologists. A child is more likely to attempt to produce words if his parents do not supply all his needs before he has tried to say anything. Parents easily get into this habit to avoid temper tantrums, but once they become confident in dealing with this behaviour, they can begin to use everyday situations to help the child to make some effort to speak. The first steps in achieving understanding and use of words, and the basis of good pronunciation, are similar for all kinds of children with severe language problems. They are described clearly in the book by Julia S. Molloy (see book list at end). In the rest of this section I shall concentrate on the difficulties which are special to autistic children.

Almost everyone tends to assume that autistic children understand more than they really do. To begin with they echo long phrases that sometimes, by coincidence, make sense. Later on they begin to pick up some simple clues from people's gestures. When they do learn to speak they sometimes acquire a large vocabulary which gives the impression that they understand a lot. If you listen to the way they make sentences and the ideas they express, it is clear that, despite the large number of words they know, their comprehension is limited. It is therefore best to use simple language when talking to an autistic child.

With a child who is only just beginning to understand, you should limit your speech to short phrases that you are sure he will understand. This is difficult to do. The normal thing is for mothers to chatter away to their children, simplifying a bit but using many extra words beyond those necessary to convey meaning. This is appropriate for a normal child because it helps him to learn new words and new grammatical structures. An autistic child on the other hand is confused by all the extra words, He is more likely to learn to come in response to 'Johnny – dinner' than to 'Come along, Johnny darling, you will have to hurry up because your dinner is getting cold'.

As time goes on the phrases can include more words. The aim is to make sure that the child understands, but to keep a tiny way ahead of him so that he can learn new words and sentences at a speed which is reasonable for him. Careful speech, limited in quantity, does not come naturally to adults. It has to be practised with conscious effort. The children are more likely to attend to words which are emphasised, so it helps to stress the important words in each sentence. Some autistic children can understand words that are sung to a tune more easily than those which are spoken. Singing words is an excellent way of increasing the child's interest in speech and willingness to try for himself.

The first words learnt are usually the names of things that the child uses. Autistic children find it especially hard to realise that many nouns refer to more than one object. They may call the dining-room chair a chair, but not realise that the same word applies to chairs of a different shape or size. Another kind of mistake occurs when they do genera-

lise but select the wrong characteristic as a basis for generalisation. One girl learnt to name a circle, but then used the
label for many other things (such as lamp-shades, steering
wheels and so on) which were circular in one dimension,
and whose real name she did not know. Parents can help
by naming things for the child, and giving him time to
repeat the words. You can never assume that a child can
name even the commonest objects unless you have specifically taught him. Normal children learn from casual
conversation which they hear all day and every day, but
autistic children seem unable to do this. On the rare occas-
sions when they do pick things up casually they are liable
to get them wrong. An autistic boy heard his father say
'It's about time I washed the car' and immediately rushed
to get his coat in preparation for a ride in the car. The
children may invent some delightful names for things when
in doubt. 'Candlestick' for mushroom, 'doggie bunny'
for kangaroo and 'make a cup of tea' for kettle are examples.
They also tend to attribute unusual meanings to words or
phrases, because of the context in which they first heard
them, such as the boy who thought that the 'middle ages'
was a time when everyone was middle-aged and the girl
who thought a pinafore dress was a garment you wore at a
performance of Gilbert and Sullivan's opera *H.M.S.
Pinafore*.

Verbs present a problem because of the way they change
in the past and future tenses. Most of the children speak in
the present tense all the time, and only the ones who learn
to speak really well are able to use tenses properly. If an
autistic child reaches the stage when he realises that the
ending 'ing' is added to make a word describing a present
action, he will apply it indiscriminately, perhaps making this
mistake for many years. He will describe a picture of a
man smoking a pipe as 'Daddy piping' or one of a child
blowing bubbles as 'Boy bubbling'.

The ability to pronounce words varies from one child

to another. Some have little trouble, and others seem to be unable to make the necessary sounds. It is best not to discourage the child from talking by paying too much attention to his pronunciation too early on. A special problem for autistic children is controlling the pitch and lilt of the voice to make it sound natural and not mechanical. A co-operative child will try to imitate the correct intonation but this practice seems to make little difference to his spontaneous speech. There is some tendency to improvement with maturity.

Reversal of pronouns makes an autistic child's speech sound odd. Once the child speaks fairly well and is not discouraged by correction, it is worth while getting him to imitate the correct phrasing. At first you will need to help him with the whole sentence ('Can *I* have a biscuit') but after a time the smallest cue can be given in a whisper, and will be sufficient to help the child say the words correctly.

The small linking words are another source of difficulty. Constant practice in everyday situations can help especially if you make use of those that interest the child. He is more likely to learn the meaning of 'in' if you say 'The dinner is *in* the oven', than if you use the word 'in' in a context that has little significance for him. His favourite possession can be placed on or under or behind a chair so that he can learn the words for positions. The teaching should be arranged to amuse the child and should stop if he becomes bored or irritable.

Autistic children often try to say things but produce the wrong words in the wrong order. They also tend to cut the number of words to the bare minimum as with the child who said 'rom-a-beans' which was eventually found to mean, 'I want to have my baked beans on toast in the sitting-room so that I can watch television while I eat'. Parents need endless patience to sort out the muddle, but this is a worth-while exercise. The children can become unhappy and discouraged if they do their best to speak and people misunderstand, become impatient, or take no notice. One girl of eleven liked to talk to people but had little verbal skill. She had made something out of her constructional toy which she showed to a visitor, saying 'Hang-it-up'. The visitor was bewildered and could not carry on the conversation, but the child's mother knew that the model represented a duffle coat on a coat-hanger, and could admire it appropriately. However, she could not make up for the visitor's lack of appreciation as she saw from her daughter's sad face. Parents have to act as interpreters so that the children can make contact with people outside the family.

The children can be taught to answer simple questions, by making them part of a game. If they know the names of common animals, the game can begin with father (or mother) saying 'The cow says moo' – the moo being said in a way that amuses the child. The next stage is for father to say 'What does the cow say?' and then answer his own question 'The cow says moo'. This can be repeated several times while the child's interest is maintained. Then the 'moo' is left off the answer, and with luck the child will supply it himself. If not, then father must continue repeating the sequence and try again later. After several sessions of this kind the child will come to supply the whole answer. Each session should be a game and stopped before it bores the child. Other similar questions can be practised, remembering to go back to the earlier ones from time to time.

Carrying simple messages is a useful skill. A child can be taught to tell his father, 'Dinner's ready, Daddy.' To begin with, he has to practise repeating the words. It is no use starting with the instruction to 'Tell Daddy that dinner's ready' because the child will echo the whole sentence as he hears it. When he can say 'Dinner's ready, Daddy' well enough, he can be taken to his father and encouraged, by whispered cues, to give the message. Father (who should

be well versed in his part too) says something like 'All right
– Daddy coming', and everyone should show the child
how well he has done. This needs to be repeated over and
over again at every dinner-time, until the child can carry
the message by himself. Eventually it may be possible to
ask the child to 'Tell Daddy that dinner is ready', but
this depends on how far his general skill with language
develops.

In the early stages it may be difficult for an autistic child
to express a preference if he is asked to choose one of two
or more things. If you say to him, 'Do you want an apple
or an orange?', he may repeat the whole sentence, or else
echo the last word ('orange') even if he really preferred the
apple. It is easier for him to make a choice if he can see the
alternatives and touch the one he wants. If you encourage
him to put his choice into words at the same time (for
example, by saying 'Apple, please') he will eventually learn
what to say.

Many young autistic children develop the habit of saying
'No' automatically, when they are asked to make too many
choices. Part of this may be due to the frustration produced
by their limited understanding, but the mischievous pleasure to be gained from annoying mother may keep the
habit going. There is little point in asking the child 'Do you
want some toast?' or 'Do you want milk or cocoa?' or
'Do you want some potato?' at every single mealtime, to
take a common example. The child should be given his
meal, in the calm expectation that he will eat it. The opportunity to choose should be arranged only when you have
the time to teach him how to make the correct reply, until
you are sure that he understands the situation well enough
to answer sensibly.

As with all other children, autistic children learn to say
'No' before 'Yes'. Questions are answered by repeating the
words of the questioner, and a child may not say 'Yes'
until he is eight or nine or even older. When he finally

does learn, he then tends to answer 'Yes' to all questions regardless of the correct reply. The proper use of 'Yes' and 'No' can be taught by asking a series of very simple questions and prompting the correct answer: 'Is your coat blue?' – 'No'. 'Is your coat green?' – 'No'. 'Is your coat brown?' – 'Yes'. Constant practice is necessary before a child can be relied upon to use the words appropriately.

Polite phrases are a useful acquisition. 'Please' and 'Thank you' can be taught by patient insistence and by suitable prompting. The child should know that he will not be given the things he wants unless he says 'Please'. 'Thank you' has first of all to be said while both you and the child together are still holding on to the desired object, so that you can release it to him only when he has said the words. In time the words will become automatic. All this may seem a lot of effort for a useless convention, but it is worth while because it affects outsiders' opinion of the child and makes him acceptable in company. It is also sensible to teach him to say 'Can I have . . .?' instead of shouting a single word. Taking things without snatching is to be encouraged. Each family has to consider the conventions of its own circle and teach the child accordingly.

Every handicapped child who may wander should have his name and address sewn to his clothes. An autistic child who can speak can learn to give his name and address if his pronunciation is reasonable. He should be taught to give it in response to many different phrases ('What is your name?', 'Where do you live?', 'Who are you?', etc.) because you cannot guarantee how he will be asked if the need arises.

If is no use pretending that talking to a child with a severe language handicap is at all easy. Attempts at conversation are laborious in the extreme and often consist of repetitions of the same simple questions and answers. One common problem is that the children become resistant to change in the things they say and may repeat the same phrase or ask the same question over and over again. The best way to deal with this is to ignore the repeated phrases, but to encourage new verbal ideas and reward them with attention and interest.

Gestures and miming are used by normal people to aid communication, and autistic children need to be encouraged to use them. They can be taught to point at things accurately instead of using a vague wave of the arm. They may also enjoy a game of pretending to do everyday actions such as brushing hair, drinking from a cup, driving a car and so on. They find these things difficult and will need patient help if they are to learn to perform even the simplest mimed actions.

iii *Toys and games*

Autistic children do not play like normal children because their handicaps prevent or severely retard the development of imagination.

Parents can help the children gain useful experience by providing the toys that usually interest babies and toddlers and showing the children how to 'play' with them. They should be encouraged to handle the nesting boxes, coloured blocks, posting boxes and so on which give the children some experience of shape, size and colour and the relationship between one object and another. Their hands need to be guided to help them fit small boxes into large ones, or to build towers of blocks. The 'play' will cease as soon as adult supervision is removed, so it is a good idea for a parent to set aside a few short periods of time each day to work with the child. Many toy-making firms give the age ranges for which various toys are suitable, and it is useful to follow these stages in the right sequence, although the children are likely to be several years behind the normal development.

Later on many autistic children enjoy jigsaw puzzles.

There are some excellent types of constructional toy on the market. If a child tends to avoid tasks involving much muscular effort, you can find constructional sets which are easily fitted together. You can also find sets which are suitable for children who are not very dextrous with their fingers.

There are now many toys which link words, sounds and pictures and some of these are ideal for a child with a language problem. In general, toys should be chosen which do not need complicated language or imagination for their enjoyment.

Autistic children have as much trouble in playing with other children as they do in playing with toys on their own. Unless they make unusually good progress they are unable to understand the purpose behind any game. They are not driven by a desire to win because they cannot grasp the concept of 'winning' with all the social awareness which this implies. By the time they are five or six years old it may be possible for parents to teach them simple games such as throwing and catching a ball which can later be played with other children. The problems of muscle control make even such a simple game difficult for an autistic child. If one adult stands behind the child, holding his arms and guiding him to catch and throw, he will eventually learn. A fairly large ball is better than a small one.

Hide-and-seek can be played when the child has sufficient understanding to know that objects still exist even if they are hidden away. It is best to begin by playing with one of the child's favourite possessions. One adult can cover the child's eyes or take him out of the room, while the other does the hiding. The child will need to be helped to search, and the object will have to be 'found' quickly at first, to avoid upsetting him by failure. As he begins to see the point, and to enjoy the surprise element, the game can go on longer and he can be encouraged to search for himself. He will tend to go back to the same place over and over again, and he will need cues to take him to other possible hiding places.

Most of the very simple games enjoyed by young children can be adapted to include an autistic child. The experience is particularly valuable if other children can join in but they need to be fairly mature in order to control their own behaviour enough to fit in with the needs of the handicapped child.

Drawing and painting are creative activities to be encouraged, but the children may have to be shown how to use pencils and paint by guiding their hands. They will begin by smearing and eating the paint until they reach a level of maturity at which they are interested in the marks they make on the paper rather than the feel of the materials. Even then many of them have little skill. It is the exceptional child who has any real ability in painting and drawing, but many of the children learn to enjoy trying to make pictures or colourful patterns.

Some autistic children are late in understanding that pictures can represent objects. One child was interested only while a picture was being drawn for her and looked away as soon as the pencil ceased moving on the paper. Another had to be shown real objects together with the pictures of them before she understood that the one represented the other. Books with plain clear pictures of everyday things are best. Cartoons and pictures with fussy detail are not much use.

The hardest problem is to keep up the autistic child's interest in any activity. A normal child plays as naturally as he breathes because his understanding of the world is always a step or so ahead of his physical achievements. He is always reaching out to anticipate the next stage of complexity. The autistic child is held back by his lack of comprehension of what life is about, and he needs constant adult supervision and encouragement to prevent him returning to his preoccupation with simple sensations.

iv *Social manners and social relationships*

Gestures and facial expressions are important in social communication. All autistic children have difficulties with this kind of language, and some of them are so handicapped that their faces appear wooden and expressionless in almost all situations. Normal people are used to estimating the feelings of others from their expressions, and often assume that autistic children are without any emotions at all. Faced with a child of this kind, most people soon give up the effort to produce a visible response, and a vicious circle is created, since the child cannot initiate contact for himself.

It is well worth while for parents to try to teach the children the outward expressions of their inner feelings. A child can be taught to shake hands if his hand is guided correctly whenever a visitor offers his hand first. It is better to teach this as a response to a proffered hand rather than encouraging the child to make the first move, since he will not understand when it is correct to do this and when not.

Positive signs of affection within the family can also be taught. Instead of allowing the child to accept a hug and a kiss passively, his own arms can be guided to return the hug. He can also be taught to hold on properly with his arms and legs when he is picked up and carried by an adult, instead of lying limply like a rag doll. Kissing can be taught in the same way, by gently guiding the child's head. If he just touches his lips on the other person's cheek, that is good enough to start with. Again it is best for the child to learn this as a response to affection from others. Once the children grasp the idea, they usually come to enjoy these social contacts, and might easily assume that this was the way to greet everyone.

Even though it may sound rather odd, one can teach a

child to smile by moving the corners of his lips. When he reaches the stage of development in which he is responsive to such teaching (perhaps around six to seven years of age, but earlier in some and later in others) parents can demonstrate different expressions on their own faces, and tell him the names, such as 'smile' and 'frown'. They can use the appropriate tone of voice, or link the names with the emotions – 'smile-happy' 'frown-angry'. A session in which the child's face is moulded into expressions while he watches a mirror can be helpful. Pictures of people with different expressions can be compared and named. The children often find this highly diverting, and laugh uproariously at their own and their parents' funny faces, and this gives the lessons a happy and positive atmosphere.

An autistic child's bodily postures or way of walking may emphasise the fact that he is handicapped. This can be corrected to some extent. He can be encouraged to swing his arms as he walks and to stand up straight without having his arms bent at the elbows or his head on one side. Sometimes the children tend to hold their mouths open, and this should be discouraged if possible. Helping to overcome these problems needs much patience and good humour. The odd postures and movements are in large part due to their immature development so the children have to try hard to stand and walk well. Irritable nagging from parents will cause justifiable resentment.

By the time a child is six or seven years old he may be able to learn to look at people instead of through or past them. This tends to come naturally with increasing age, but can be encouraged. It may be necessary to start with sessions in which his father or mother gently holds the child's head, and attracts his visual attention. The way to success is to obtain a child's co-operation by making faces that amuse him, or whispering, or singing a favourite song. In short the teaching should be pleasant for the child. One game that often makes a child laugh while encouraging him to look in your eyes is to touch noses and then twist your head so that a funny visual effect is created by the way your eyes move.

The children's interest in other people grows with experience. Friends and relations can help especially if the child's handicaps are explained to them. People who regularly call at the door are often friendly and understanding. The child can be taught to answer the door when told and to say 'Hallo'. (If you live in an area where not all callers are desirable it is best to teach him not to answer the door automatically when the bell rings, but to wait for your instructions.)

It is easier for these children to relate to adults than to other children, especially those of the same age or younger. This is probably because adults are able to adapt themselves to the child, whereas other children do not have the necessary insight, and do not modify their behaviour. The exceptions are some normal children who have a handicapped brother and sister of their own. If the situation is handled well by their parents, they may be remarkably good at interacting with an autistic child. There is not much that parents can do to make it easier for their autistic child to get on better with other children, except to help him join in with simple games. Most autistic children with moderate or severe handicaps will always need adult supervision and guidance whenever they are with a group of normal children. The situation must never be allowed to degenerate so that the autistic child becomes aggressive, or else withdraws and wanders away on his own. He must be protected against the occasional normal child who reacts to a handicapped person by bullying and teasing. Autistic children cannot defend themselves and do not learn to do so through experience. They have neither the verbal wit nor the physical skills to hold their own among their peers.

So far I have concentrated upon ways of encouraging social mixing. The other side of the picture can be seen in some children who make good progress. They may become over-friendly and sociable, in an immature way, and fail to discriminate between people they know and complete strangers. One girl of ten, who had had quite severe visual as well as speech handicaps, tended to assume that people she met in the street were people she knew. She would rush up to them with a joyful greeting, to their utter amazement. Her parents had to restrain her and explain many times over that she must not talk to people in the street unless her parents made the first move. She was most upset at first, but the phase passed after a few months. There is no easy answer, since one naturally does not want to discourage a spontaneous friendliness which one has spent so long in encouraging. However, I have not met any children who have become withdrawn again because their over-friendliness has had to be curbed.

v *Outings and social occasions*

When they are under four or five years old, autistic children, especially those with marked visual problems, tend to find crowds and bustle confusing and frightening. This makes it difficult to take them into shops, to parties or even into crowded streets. As they grow older and their handicaps lessen, most of the children begin to enjoy outings, especially since they have so little creative play with which to occupy themselves.

In the transition stage, when fear is receding and enjoyment is growing, expeditions should be carefully planned. First of all you should arrange to keep them fairly short, and not too far from home, so that you can easily remove the child if the situation proves too much for him. You have to try different kinds of outing. If one is not a success, then leave it for a while and try again later. A visit to the zoo, with lively, noisy, smelly animals may terrify an autistic child of three, but give great pleasure to one of seven years.

With a young child a certain amount of equipment is necessary. Food may have to be taken if a restaurant is a problem, because hunger can make a child more difficult to manage. A pot may be necessary if public lavatories frighten the child. A damp sponge and a towel or paper tissues are invaluable aids. A favourite toy, or small object which does not look too odd to strangers, should be allowed, to give the child a link with his home. The most important preparation of all is basic training in reasonable social manners, so that parents can feel relaxed, and the whole family, including the child, can enjoy the outing.

Later on, outings can become longer and more complicated. It helps the child to tell him in advance (in simple words) and to draw pictures of where he is going and what will happen. Most theatre and film shows are of no interest to autistic children, but they may enjoy musicals where much of the action is singing and dancing, with few spoken lines. Their pleasure is considerably increased if they can hear a record of the music played before they see the show, so that they can learn the tunes. Cartoon films with music are usually a success. If the child can attend private film shows first it is easier to teach him that he must not talk or wander around during the performance. The children may be delighted to join in with clapping and laughing even though they do not understand the joke. Their humour tends to be concrete. Slapstick comedy with people falling over and throwing water around goes down well, so some old silent films will appeal.

Older autistic children usually like to go to parties although they may join in very little. One boy was sad when his sisters were invited to parties without him. The hosts had not realised that in his own quiet way he was enjoying himself. Parents, who so often have to stand between the world and their child, need to overcome any diffidence they feel, and explain to friends and relations, so that the child has as much social life as possible.

vi *Travel and holidays*

Once past the difficult early years, and once special fears of buses, cars or trains have been overcome, many autistic children thoroughly enjoy travelling. Some parents even find that their children behave better on a journey than on any other occasion.

Apart from the actual journey, holidays may be difficult. A young autistic child may be bewildered by new surroundings, and may never settle during the whole period away from home. Many families do not take a vacation, or else try to arrange temporary residential care for the child while the rest of the family goes away.

This problem can often be overcome with time and patience. Careful teaching of social behaviour and basic co-operation and obedience eventually enables the family to live a more normal life. The most easily managed type of holiday (apart from staying with an understanding friend or relative) is to rent a small house or chalet for the family, away from other people, and to cater for oneself. Some of the autistic child's favourite possessions should be taken to make him feel secure. The days can be planned to include some activity to keep him amused and happy.

When a child is reasonably well behaved, staying a night in a hotel can be tried. Once this is accomplished other kinds of holidays become possible. Some parents have taken their children abroad and the whole family has benefited from the experience. The same rules apply whatever expedition is planned. These are: be consistent and firm in social training; prepare the child in advance through words and pictures; increase the scope of the expeditions gradually (that is, don't move from one afternoon in the local park straight to three weeks in a hotel in Italy); and take his favourite clothes and toys with you to preserve the child's link with the familiar and the secure.

What parents can do 119

vii *Memory and anticipation – the practical use of pictures, reading and writing*

Autistic children have difficulty in grasping the concept of time. The meanings of the words 'minutes', 'hours', 'days', 'weeks' or 'yesterday', 'tomorrow', 'next year' are hard to understand and to learn. This affects the children's social behaviour in different ways at different stages of development. In the early years the problem shows itself as an inability to wait. This is common to all young children, but, as usual, it goes on much longer in an autistic child. Some of them begin to scream if made to wait more than a second for their food, for a walk, a ride in the car or anything else that they want. An orderly routine reduces the occasions on which this happens, but the children can be taught, in gradual stages, to wait in moderate patience. It is easier to do this once the child pays some attention to words. When he is seated in his special chair for dinner you can say to him 'Dinner in a minute' or 'Dinner soon' or whatever phrase you would use naturally, as long as it is fairly short. You wait a few seconds and then give him his food. The waiting time can be lengthened very slowly, always using the phrase which reassures him that dinner really *is* just coming. Once a child has learnt to wait for a while he is easier to take out, and into other people's homes.

The lack of understanding of time also shows itself in an inability to consider the past or to anticipate the future. Parents often say how sad it is that their children do not seem to recall happy events, or look forward to enjoyable occasions, because this means they lack two of the major sources of pleasure in life. The children can be helped to overcome this handicap, at home and at school, if regular events that they enjoy are planned and talked about, before and after they have occurred. The events, which can be small and simple like having something extra nice for tea, should be arranged frequently enough for the child to be able to remember.

Pictures and diagrams are invaluable in this connection, once the children's visual understanding has reached an appropriate level. A calendar can be drawn, with each day represented by a square in a row of seven for one week. The name of each day can be written in, and then a little drawing of the central event of each day put into the square. The child can cross off yesterday's square (while you say 'yesterday all gone' or something similar), then the events of today can be described with the aid of the picture. Some children manage to grasp the idea of a day and a week, and then a whole month can be drawn. Events inside a day can be placed in time, 'before dinner', 'after dinner', 'before tea', and 'after tea' and so on. Later on, the words morning and afternoon and evening can be taught by linking them to meal times.

If a special outing is planned, pictures can be drawn to show what will happen, using the appropriate words at the same time. Photographs or, better still, slides which can be projected on to a screen, can be taken on holidays, or trips to the seaside, and these can be shown to the child afterwards and the story told in simple words. It is a good idea to have pictures or slides of each member of the family, friends, and household pets, so that the child can look at them and name them.

In general an autistic child can learn more from a picture than from words, because, almost always, the difficulties of visual understanding are less severe and improve faster than those of auditory comprehension. The children find it hard to follow a sequence of events and here a diagram can be invaluable. One girl was told that she was going out shopping with mother, then to a restaurant and finally to a film show. She repeated this sequence time and time again, each time getting it wrong. It is not at all surprising that children with this problem become anxious, and go on and on worrying about it until they get it right. Finally this little girl was shown a picture with the shop at the top, the restaurant underneath, and the cinema under that, and her finger was guided to touch each one in turn in the correct sequence. This satisfied her completely. (It would not have worked if she had still been in the stage in which left-right, back-front and up-down were hopelessly confused.) A boy of ten was helped to understand words like second, minute, hour and day when his mother drew lines of different length to demonstrate the relationship of the different time periods.

A fair number of autistic children learn to read, in the sense that they can pronounce words they see written down, but hardly any of them have much comprehension of reading material. They therefore do not read for pleasure or interest. One way parents at home can help a child to feel that reading can be worth the effort is to prepare a book of 'stories' about the child's own everyday life, illustrated with drawings or photographs. It can be as simple as one sentence on each page. 'Tom get up', 'Tom eating breakfast', 'Tom going to shop with Mummy', each with its own picture. A seaside holiday book can be made in the same way.

The same idea applies when encouraging a child to practise writing. An autistic girl of twelve began to enjoy writing words when she realised that she could make a list of the things she wanted when shopping. Developing this skill then helped her in another way. She became tense and anxious for several days before a special event because she hated waiting. Then she began to write down a few words about whatever event she was anticipating. This seemed to reassure her that it really would happen in the end, and she was able to relax and look forward with pleasure.

Normal children enjoy bedtime stories before settling

down to sleep. Autistic children do not understand language well enough to appreciate fiction, but they often do enjoy it if mother or father goes over the events of the day. A 'story' of this kind, perhaps followed by a favourite song, makes a cosy family routine with which to say good night, as well as helping the development of language and memory.

PHYSICAL HEALTH

Lack of speech makes it difficult for an autistic child to show when he does not feel well, or to indicate the site of any pain. Parents have to observe his behaviour as carefully as they can, and notice any signs of illness such as extra fretfulness, lack of appetite, lethargy, rashes or a feverish flush. It is useful to teach a child a few words that he can use if he is in pain or discomfort. 'Throat sore' or 'leg hurt', give some guide to what is wrong. A small girl liked to have an adhesive plaster put on any minor injury, and when she had an attack of tonsillitis the first sign was that she said to her mother, 'Poor froat – put plaster on.'

Many autistic children furiously resist attempts at physical examination. It is possible to overcome this by playing a game of 'examining like a doctor' so that the child becomes accustomed to a hand on his tummy and the bell of a stethoscope on his chest. It also helps to practise opening and closing the eyes and the mouth when told (the words 'close' and 'open' are often confused by the children). If possible, the child should get to know the family doctor as a friend before he has any physical illness, so that he is less apprehensive when he does need treatment.

Handicapped children who have problems with chewing and with mouth and tongue movements are particularly liable to tooth decay. They are given much soft food, and they do not use their tongues to remove scraps of food from between their teeth. Careful and regular toothbrushing is essential. An electric toothbrush if used properly cleans effectively, and also helps the child to become used to the feeling of vibration, which is similar to that of some dental instruments. Regular visits to the dentist are necessary, and should begin well before any treatment is needed. A dentist needs patience and a way with children which will enable him to teach an autistic child to sit in the chair and allow his teeth to be inspected and cleaned. Some children become so used to dental procedures that they will accept small fillings without an anaesthetic. Others, however, will need a general anaesthetic for such procedures.

If an autistic child has to go into hospital it is better for him if his mother can accompany him. He needs her reassurance and comfort even more than a normal child of the same age. The doctors and nurses will need the mother's help. She can explain things to the child and tell him what he has to do. She can also tell the staff of her child's needs since he usually cannot convey his meaning to strangers. The doctor and ward sister may appreciate some information about autistic children if they have not treated a child of this kind before.* In this situation a mother has to hide her natural anxiety, present a calm and confident front to her child, and co-operate fully with the medical and nursing staff, so that the child feels as happy and relaxed as possible.

A doctor or dentist who is treating a child should be told if he is receiving any drugs, such as sleeping tablets or daytime sedatives. This is particularly important if an anaesthetic (local or general) has to be given. Autistic children may be muddled and confused when they wake up from an anaesthetic, and may need a sedative to calm them down. They will be helped and comforted if a parent or another familiar person is there to give reassurance.

Among the drugs which may be given to autistic children

* The British National Society for Autistic Children publishes a brief information leaflet for this purpose.

to lessen overactive and difficult behaviour there are some which make the skin sensitive to sunlight. This may cause swelling and a rash if the child spends any time in the sunshine. This can be prevented by avoiding the sun, and wearing long sleeves and a shady hat. Your doctor will tell you if any tablets he gives your child are likely to have this effect, and he will advise on special precautions.

PROBLEMS OF ADOLESCENCE

These depend upon how much progress each individual child has made by the time he has reached the years of adolescence. At one end of the scale, some children change so little that they still have the same problems as those of the young autistic child. At the other end, some children are able to talk and understand fairly well and their difficulties have something in common with those of the normal teenager.

i *Immature social responses*

I have already mentioned this problem in various sections of this book. The extra difficulty presented in adolescence is that the immature behaviour and naive comments attract far more attention in someone who is physically almost adult than they do in a younger child. Parents have to continue to teach general rules of conduct, and also the applications of these rules to any particular situation. They can arrange suitable opportunities for social mixing with other normal adolescents who are sensible and understanding. Suitable companions have to be chosen with some care, because some normal adolescents of a mischievous turn of mind could take advantage of an autistic child's naive innocence and passivity, and lead him into trouble.

Because of their immaturity, most autistic adolescents

do not have the feelings of rebellion against their parents which are seen in normal young people. They do not go in for demonstrations, for drug-taking, for peculiar forms of dress, or any of the outward signs of protest. The usual complaint of parents of an autistic adolescent is that he has very little drive to do anything. Children who have been overactive often become underactive in their adolescent years. When rebelliousness does occur it is likely to be a childish irritability and stubbornness, rather than a determined, sustained protest. This can be trying to manage, and it is not easy to combine the necessary patience and understanding of the teenager's handicaps with an attempt to treat him as much like an adult as is possible in view of his limitations and need for protection and security. A desire to be independent may come in adult life to some people who have been autistic as children, and who have developed enough to have some concept of what independence means. When this happens, all that the parents can do is to allow their son or daughter to make the experiment of living away from home, but to be ready to give whatever help is necessary if things go wrong, without appearing to be over-protective.

ii *Sexual development*

Puberty is usually not delayed in autistic children, even though they often look younger than their actual age. Interest in sex tends to be on an immature level. Some of the children develop a childish curiosity about their own and other people's bodies, and may innocently try to undress other children. The fact that this is 'not done' is one more of the rules which they have to learn.

Masturbation can be a problem in autistic children. Their lack of social sense may mean that they masturbate in public, especially if they are unoccupied and bored. This should be discouraged in the same way as any other socially unde-

sirable behaviour, not because masturbation is in any way
harmful, but because other people do not accept a child
who behaves in this way.

Menstruation usually begins within the same age range
as with normal girls. Special waterproof plastic covers for
sanitary pads can be bought. A routine for changing pads
regularly should be followed until the girl can cope for
herself. Sometimes an autistic child will talk about her
periods to people she meets. Although it is an excellent idea
to adopt an open and matter-of-fact attitude towards the facts
of life, nevertheless it is necessary to teach a child discretion
in these matters because there are still many people who
are shocked or embarrassed by these subjects. You can
explain that the time to make comments or ask questions
is when alone with Mother, and not when other people
are around.

Asking questions about conception and birth presuppo-
ses a reasonable level of language development, so it is
only a small minority of autistic adolescents who will even
ask their parents about these matters. Answers should be
frank, but simple enough for the child's understanding.
A few adolescents may say that they intend to get married
and have children, but people who have been autistic as
children rarely seem to have any drive towards finding a
regular boy or girl friend, or towards adult sexual activity,
although they may show a naive preference and physical
affection for the opposite sex. In any case they almost
always lack the social skills to attract another boy or girl.
Some parents worry because their autistic daughter is
over-friendly to strangers, and is easily led. Usually, however, it is fairly easy to supervise such a child, and her
social contacts. One or two cases have been reported
(without much documentary evidence) of people with
autistic behaviour as children who grew up and married,
but they seem to have grown out of the symptoms completely by the time of adolescence. In these circumstances

it is difficult to know if they really did have early childhood autism.

iii *Insight*

It is difficult to know how far young autistic children are aware of their handicaps. They certainly feel intense distress and unhappiness when they are frustrated or confused by their environment, but whether or not they compare themselves with other children is difficult to estimate. It is unlikely that the majority of the children can do this because they are limited by their language handicap. Sometimes, however, an autistic child will stand on the edge of a group of normal children and watch their play with a look of wistful longing and intense sadness.

The children who show marked improvement are likely to have a fair amount of insight by the time they reach adolescence. They may express this in their own way. One boy used to say sadly, over and over again, 'Can't do it. Got no brain.' A girl of fourteen who was able to talk well once asked her mother, 'Mummy when God made me, why didn't he make me quite right?' Other children ask why they are different from their brothers and sisters. When an autistic adolescent begins to think about this problem he may become miserable and depressed. He will need comfort and reassurance from his parents and family. It will also help him to point out the things that he can do well, and to explain that everyone has problems and handicaps.

Occasionally an adolescent who is concerned about his handicaps will try to do something to show that he is normal, and this may have disastrous results. One young man thought he would improve his health if he took up running, so he ran for miles in bitterly cold weather in his vest and pants, and was found in an exhausted condition a very long way from home. It may not be possible to predict, and therefore prevent, this kind of impulsive behaviour. It is also impossible to shield a bright autistic adolescent from the knowledge that he is not the same as others. What one can do is to offer continued affection and concern, and to help him find some occupation which can give him the feeling that he has a role in life.

iv *Employment problems*

A small number of autistic adults manage to work in open employment. The occupations they have followed cover a wide range and include work in mathematics, office work, piano-tuning, bricklaying, street-cleaning and domestic work. In every case a sympathetic and knowledgeable employer was the most important factor in allowing the person to settle down into a routine. There are a number of problems which can cause difficulties in finding suitable employment. The language disorder excludes work which involves good conversational ability, social interaction or high skill in reading. The lack of flexibility means that work where instructions are complicated and methods change frequently is likely to be unsuitable. Some autistic adults may still be sensitive to noises and bright lights and may be unable to tolerate these conditions in a factory. They tend to be upset if people are impatient or irritable, or if anyone shouts loudly. When they start work they need someone to explain every little detail, to show them the cloakroom and toilets, how to collect lunch from the canteen, what time to stop work and so on, and someone to keep an eye open to make sure everything goes smoothly. The journey to work may have unexpected snags. With public transport there is the risk that the usual bus or train may be late or cancelled, and this may produce confusion and distress. A parent, hostel warden or other guardian usually has to make sure that an autistic adult looks after himself, has regular meals, and changes his clothes as often as is necessary.

On the positive side, those who can fit into open employment are hard-working and conscientious. Once they have learned the rules they apply them with meticulous accuracy. (This can have its negative side, since striving for perfect accuracy may slow up the work below a level which is acceptable.) They are completely honest and open, and usually popular with their colleagues, once their handicaps are understood and accepted.

The majority of autistic adults need sheltered conditions, in which a wide range of work is available so that a suitable job can be found to fit each individual person's special skills. Some people with experience of the problems of employing autistic adolescents recommend that work should be organised to allow a change of task several times during the day, to avoid boredom. Many of the more handicapped autistic adults need much supervision and repetition of instructions to keep them working, because lethargy and lack of initiative is a major problem. The effort to provide occupation is well worth while because constructive activity makes the odd behaviour less obvious, and encourages continued improvement.

HOME OR RESIDENTIAL CARE

All parents have to consider whether they should keep a handicapped child at home or try to place him in residential care. The question is likely to arise at various times, such as in the early difficult stages; when other siblings are born; when parents are ill or become elderly and infirm. Good residential care is extremely difficult to find, so keeping a child at home may be the only alternative open to the parents.

There is, in my opinion, no doubt that a good, secure, loving family is the best environment for an autistic child. If parents want to keep their child at home, and the family is close enough and stable enough to take the strain, they should be given every encouragement and help. There is nothing to be gained from admission to a hospital unit in these circumstances. The diagnosis can be made on an out-patient basis unless there are special reasons for a brief stay as an in-patient. A day school should be found if at all possible. Weekly or termly boarding may have to be considered if no day school is available in the neighbourhood.

This is the ideal provision, but there are many reasons why residential care might have to be found. One or other parent may have a chronic illness, there may be only one parent to cope with the family, the siblings may seem to be suffering, or the housing situation may make caring for an overactive child almost impossible, to give just a few examples. Parents have to consider all facets of the problem and make up their own minds. They should have the benefit of expert advice, but in the end the decision is theirs alone. Residential care should be organised so that they can maintain contact with their child and do not feel that he has been entirely taken out of their care.

Autistic adults who no longer have parents or other relatives with whom they can live, will, in most cases, need a home to be provided for them. Suggestions for types of residential accommodation will be made in a later section.

10

The autistic child's family

THE PROBLEMS OF BROTHERS AND SISTERS

It is hard to find evidence of the effect on the brothers and sisters of having a handicapped child in the family. Some studies of different kinds of handicaps have been done, and have given conflicting results. It seems that some normal children are adversely affected by a handicapped sibling, whereas others manage well and perhaps benefit from the experience in the end. The reasons for these different responses have not been worked out, although it is fair to say that a united family with parents who accept and understand the handicapped child gives the best chance to all its children.

Obviously, however brothers and sisters respond to the experience, they do face a number of special problems. Perhaps the hardest thing for them is that their parents have to give so much attention to the handicapped child (particularly one who is autistic) that the others do not have their fair share. This is worst for a child who is near in age to the autistic child, and parents have to be aware of this danger and do their best to give their normal children plenty of affection and interest. If it is possible to arrange for some domestic help, this may enable the parents to organise their time more easily.

An older normal child of school age, with a young autistic brother or sister, does not suffer quite so much from lack of attention, but he may feel unable to bring his friends home to play. It is easier for him if his parents encourage and welcome his friends (however tired and harassed they may feel) and make sure that there is somewhere where they can play in peace. It is best to explain frankly and simply about the child's handicaps and to answer the questions of the brothers and sisters and their friends in as calm and relaxed a manner as possible.

A destructive autistic child may break his brothers' and sisters' toys. Normal children naturally find this hard to bear. They need to have a special place to lock their precious possessions out of harm's way. Parents should teach their autistic child, as soon as they can, not to touch any toys except his own. They should replace all damaged toys if they possibly can. If a normal child is reassured that his rights are being respected, he will accept the occasional loss of a possession with better grace, and will be more willing to play with his autistic brother and help him to use toys.

A normal child may worry about the possibility of developing symptoms like his handicapped sibling. He will not understand why his brother or sister is different, and he may have all kinds of alarming fears and fantasies. Parents need to be sensitive to these feelings. They can help by their calm acceptance of all their children, their willingness to discuss and to explain, and their love and reassurance.

An adolescent may worry about the possibility of having an autistic child himself when he marries. Very little is known about the chance of a recurrence of early childhood autism within a family. A few families have more than one autistic child, and in other cases a brother or a sister has some other mental or physical handicap. Sometimes there is a family history of left-handedness and difficulty with talking, reading or writing, or of mild eccentricity and lack of sociability in aunts, uncles or cousins. No studies have been done to show if these problems occur more often in the relatives of autistic children than in the general popu-lation. If autism is inherited, it is not passed on as a straight-

forward Mendelian dominant or recessive characteristic.
The risk, if any, is obviously not a very marked one, otherwise it would have been noted in the now extensive
literature on the condition.

Some normal children enjoy teaching an autistic child and
can involve an autistic brother or sister in a variety of
activities. It is also common to find that normal children
with a handicapped sibling develop an air of maturity
beyond their years. Parents have to beware of placing too
much responsibility on the shoulders of their normal off-
spring, and make sure that they have plenty of time for
ordinary childish pursuits, without having their play inter-
rupted by the autistic child.

Discussing the difficulties met by the brothers and sisters
underlines the importance of teaching an autistic child
reasonable social behaviour. There is no reason why the
child's basic handicaps or his retardation should have any
lasting adverse effect on his siblings. All the problems
arise because of the secondary behaviour disorders which
disrupt family life, and these secondary problems can and
should be minimised with proper management.

THE PROBLEMS OF PARENTS

Parents have to cope with a series of problems some of
which are practical and some of which are emotional.
Many of these are common to parents of mentally handicapped children in general, while others are special to the
families of autistic children.

GENERAL PROBLEMS

The parents of any chronically handicapped child have to
undergo a complete change of attitude when they first
learn the truth, and this is a painful process. Like all

parents they start off with the expectation that they have a normal baby who will grow up like everyone else. They have to adjust to the fact that all their hopes and plans for their child's future (and to some extent their own future as well) will have to be changed. It is hard for them to resist the feeling that somehow they have failed. Physical or mental abnormalities seem to trigger off feelings of shame and guilt which are quite irrational, but which have to be anticipated and understood.

The immediate practical problems with a mentally retarded child are those of greatly prolonged baby and toddler stages, often with problems of feeding and general health, plus difficult behaviour as well.

Once school age is reached, the parents see other children entering the normal school system, and their own child going to a special school. In some areas, these special units are referred to by unpleasant names by other children (and some adults) and the shame and sadness, which may have faded a little, come into the foreground again. School holidays are often a problem because the mother has to organise her day so that she can cope with a bored and difficult child as well as doing the housework.

Dependence on the parents usually continues into adolescence and adult life. Difficult behaviour is likely to become less marked, but any tendency to aggressiveness is much harder to cope with in a fully grown adult than in a small child. Even if schooling was provided throughout childhood, a suitable occupation may be hard to find, epecially if the handicaps are too severe to allow placement in open employment. Handicapped people are bored and miserable when unoccupied and their symptoms may become more obvious in these circumstances.

Parents always worry about what will happen after they die. If their handicapped child lives a limited but happy life at home, parents find it hard to bear the thought that he will pass the remainder of his days in an institution.

I have already mentioned the problems of the other normal children in a family, which naturally cause the parents concern. Other relatives may provide help and support, but sometimes their attitudes can be less constructive. They may feel that a handicapped child brings shame on the whole family (disregarding the fact that all families have handicapped relatives somewhere in their histories). They may try to lay the blame on one parent or the other, or else criticise the decisions the parents make concerning home or residential care and their methods of teaching and managing the child. Worst of all, they may reject the child and try to avoid seeing him or involving him in family affairs, visits or outings.

Having a handicapped child tends to limit the family's social life. It may be difficult to find a baby-sitter, especially for an older child who has disturbed behaviour. Sometimes parents avoid taking their handicapped child out with them, because his appearance or his behaviour mark him as abnormal. They may shrink from other people's stares and comments, which they tend to exaggerate because of their sensitivity. It can happen that a family becomes almost completely isolated, dropping contacts with friends, never going out together and never having visitors in the home. In this case it is true to say that a handicapped child has led to a handicapped family.

Handicapped children may mean an extra financial burden. Laundering sheets and nappies, special food or special clothing, replacing any damage done if the child is destructive, can be expensive items. Extra domestic help, plus a baby-sitter long past the age when they are necessary for normal children, may be essential for the survival of the family. The burden becomes worse with increasing age and size. Parents may have to buy clothes and food for adolescents and adults who are unable to earn any money. A few countries give adequate allowances to disabled people but most do not, and parents have to cope as best they can.

Parents whose children are in residential care have re-
duced but not eliminated their problems. They may wonder
if they have made the right decision. They may have the
child home for weekends and holidays, with the prospect
of a sad parting each time he returns to the residential
unit or hospital. These intermittent visits may in some ways
be harder for the parents and siblings than if they are used to
having the child home the whole time. The distress is
particularly acute if the only residential care available is
in a large institution where individual attention can never
be provided.

SPECIAL PROBLEMS

Autistic children, unless they have some additional handicap
affecting their appearance, look normal, and are often very
attractive. The diagnosis is not usually made before the age
of two or later and parents go through a long period of
doubt in which they have a background of nagging anxiety.
that their child is not normal, but which they try to push
out of their minds. They reassure themselves because his
physical development gives no cause for alarm and every
now and again he does something so skilfully that everyone
is sure that he is really intelligent. The time comes eventually
when the anxiety is seen to be justified, and expert help
is sought. By this time they may have swung so often
between hope and despair that they may find the truth hard
to accept. The delay in diagnosis also means that the child
has developed many secondary behaviour problems which
might have been avoided if his handicaps had been understood from birth.

Autism is a comparatively rare condition. Unless they
are put in touch with other people in the same situation,
parents tend to feel that they are alone in the world, and
that no one else has a child like theirs. They feel lost and
unable to decide what to do for the best because nothing

they have ever learnt about children gives them any idea
how to deal with the symptoms of autism. They usually
try one approach to the child after another, but give each
one up as they do not know how long they ought to persist
in order to have any effect. Some parents do find their own
way out of this dilemma, but others never find any satis-
factory solution unless given the right kind of help.

In the past some professional workers have advised
parents against contacting other families with an autistic
child. This was because of the theory that the parents themselves were in some way responsible for their child's behaviour. This meant that the usual guilt and shame felt by
a parent of any handicapped child was magnified for the
parents of autistic children to the detriment of the whole
family. Fortunately there has been a considerable swing
away from this kind of theory in recent years.

The child's aloofness in the early years causes much distress. Parents tend to feel useless and unwanted. The later
development of affection and friendliness when it occurs
is a source of pleasure and satisfaction. Disturbed behaviour
and episodes of screaming are especially common in autistic
as compared with other handicapped children, and parents
find it particularly hard because there seems to be no way
of comforting or helping the child.

Acceptance of handicap is necessary for proper teaching
and management, but this is harder to achieve with an
autistic child than, for example, with a mongol child,
because autistic children frequently have some non-verbal
skills. Parents often feel desperately that if they tried hard
enough they could help their child to be completely normal.
If this leads to a refusal to face facts the results can be disastrous for both the parents and the child.

Another problem arises from the children's normal
appearance. When they show disturbed behaviour in the
street stangers tend to feel that the children are thoroughly
spoilt. They stare and criticise, instead of showing sympathy

as they would with a child who looked severely handicapped. This may sound a trivial problem but many parents know just how infuriating this can be. The naive behaviour of the older child and adolescent is also made to appear that much odder in contrast with his look of complete normality.

To add to all the other special problems, parents have a particularly difficult time when trying to find suitable residential care for the autistic child. Services in all countries are few and far between because interest in early childhood autism has developed so much later than that in children with other handicaps.

REDUCING THE STRESSES AND STRAINS

Unity within the family is a major factor in coping successfully with the strain of raising a handicapped child. In the early years, before the facts have been fully accepted, and when the problems are at their height, it is important to avoid the temptation to blame the other partner for the child's handicaps. It does no good, and a lot of harm, to criticise each other for mishandling the child, or to search for hypothetical evidence that the condition was inherited from one or other side of the family. A series of sleepless nights and terrible days can try the patience of a saint, but the effort of remaining calm and reasonable is well worth while. Keeping one's temper and refusing to nag or become irritable all become easier if worked at consistently. Good family relations have a beneficial effect on the child's behaviour, partly because any child is happier and easier to manage within a united family, and partly because the proper handling of difficult behaviour demands a consistent approach from both parents who must back each other's decisions in front of the child, and reserve questions and discussions on methods for when they are alone together.

A sense of humour is also a great help at these times.

Many of the things that autistic children do and say are extremely funny, even if trying at the time they happen, and it does one good to laugh at them in retrospect.

Training and teaching an autistic child is time-consuming. Combining this with bringing up normal children as well sounds like an impossible feat. The only solution seems to be to organise a routine so that the normal children and the handicapped child each have some of the parents' attention each day. A short session with father or mother which comes regularly each day is better than two or three hours together and then nothing more for several days. The parents should not forget themselves in their timetable. They need some rest and relaxation away from the family in order to preserve their sense of proportion. If their horizons are limited to the daily life of the handicapped child, excluding all else, no one benefits, least of all the child himself.

Looking at the parents' problems, an outsider might wonder how they survive and why so many of them positively want to have their child living at home. The attachment between parents and child grows through the daily experience of caring and being cared for. Despite all the difficulties, the very weakness and dependence of a handicapped child often makes this bond especially strong. In the early years this may be the only reason why the parents persevere. Then, as the child's handicaps begin to lessen, each tiny step forward is a new joy, which because it is so long in coming is even more rewarding than the rapid progress of a normal child. This is especially so if the parents feel that they themselves have contributed to these advances. Autistic children have a specially appealing quality about them, because they are so innocent, so fundamentally gentle, and so vulnerable. When they improve enough to be able to participate in special occasions, their whole-hearted enjoyment is a pleasure to see. Once the children reach the stage at which they can return affection, the parents are usually quite sure that all they have been through was well worth while.

Families of handicapped children need help and support from professional workers, including teachers, doctors and social workers, to advise and help with each problem as it comes along. Most of this advice should be on the practical level so that a plan of action can be followed. Many of the parents' emotional problems recede into the background once they have a positive role to play. When they know what to do, and when they are reassured that their efforts will produce results in the end, they become less anxious, and better able to manage. They are also much more likely to co-operate with a professional worker who gives good sound advice based on experience. In the next section I shall discuss the kinds of services that would help both parents and children.

11

Services for autistic children

The details of plans for services for handicapped children depend upon the social patterns of the countries and local areas concerned. However, it is possible to give some general suggestions for services which would cover many of the needs of autistic children and adults.

DIAGNOSTIC AND ASSESSMENT CENTRES

A comprehensive diagnostic and assessment centre would deal with many different kinds of handicaps. The assessment of mental handicaps would be carried out by a team including a psychiatrist, paediatrician, neurologist, psychologist, teacher, nurse and social worker. The results would be used to help plan education and eventually employment. Reassessments should be done at intervals, so that the child's progress could be watched and new teaching methods tried if necessary. As much of the work as possible should be done on an out-patient basis. If in-patient admission is necessary, mothers should be able to come in with their children. If home circumstances prevent this, visiting should be completely unrestricted and the mother encouraged to feed, wash and play with her child rather than give these tasks to a nurse.

One of the most important functions of units of this kind would be the provision of advice and help to parents, on both practical and emotional problems, including the opportunity for training in methods of managing disturbed behaviour. Some centres are being developed in this country, but it is still very difficult for the majority of parents to obtain the advice and help they need.

Such assessment centres should be linked to appropriate educational and medical services. They are of little or no use unless these other services are available. Many parents feel that the provision of schools for the whole of childhood and adolescence is the first priority and that diagnostic centres should be developed as part of a comprehensive service.

PRE-SCHOOL UNITS

In recent years, some playgroups, nursery schools and day nurseries have started to accept handicapped, including autistic, children from 2 or 3 years old until school age. This has proved to be of help to the children by introducing them to the company of other children and helping them to learn self care and social skills. A service of this kind is also much appreciated by the parents, especially the mother, who has some relief from the constant care of the child in his most difficult years.

SCHOOLS

Autistic children need to be able to attend a suitable school from the age of five, or in many cases even earlier than this, up to late adolescence. There has been much argument as to whether the children do best if mixed with normal children, other kinds of handicapped children, or in special schools dealing only with autistic children. In my opinion the evidence so far suggests that they do best in a structured environment, in which they are given individual attention, later on being taught in small groups of three or four or more as they progress. The teaching methods must be adapted for children with severe language handicaps. The scope of education provided has to be wide enough to help children throughout the whole range of intelligence, from the above average to the severely sub-normal. On the whole it is easier to provide these conditions in special schools, and more difficult (though not impossible) to provide them in schools for normal or other handicapped children. Those with mild handicaps, and those who make good progress after a period of time in a special school, may manage to mix with other kinds of children and continue to learn in their company, but the majority need special education throughout their school life.

RESIDENTIAL ACCOMMODATION

If a child cannot live at home, it may be possible to find him a place in a residential school. This may work well, but some families find the school holidays too great a strain. When full time residential accommodation is necessary, small units run on family lines appear to be the best solution. The child can go to the local special school every day in the same way as if he were living at home. Given enough staff with appropriate experience, some autistic children could live in a family unit of this kind, together with children who had other kinds of handicaps.

Adolescents and adults who were autistic as children also need residential accommodation, when they can no longer live with their own families. Hostels for the handicapped within the local community could accept autistic people who have made sufficient progress to fit in. There may also be a case for some hostels which specialise in autistic adults and those with related handicaps.

A few village communities for handicapped people have been developed by voluntary bodies. Some autistic adolescents and adults have been accepted in 'villages' for those with various kinds of mental retardation. A sheltered community specifically for autistic adolescents and adults has just been opened (August 1974) with the support of the National Society for Autistic Children, and is the first one of its kind.

There are some autistic children, and adults whose handicaps and behaviour problems are so severe that they could not be accepted in a hostel or sheltered community. The only provision available for them is a place in a sub-normality hospital. Many of these hospitals suffer because of the legacy from the past of unsuitable buildings and the present shortage of staff. However, some of them are interested in developing facilities for autistic people and other special groups. This is a most welcome development to be encouraged and supported by parents, professional workers and voluntary helpers.

HOSPITAL TREATMENT UNITS

There is as yet no medical treatment for early childhood autism. Most help therefore comes from an educational rather than a medical approach.

Admission to a hospital unit may be required in certain special situations, apart from the obvious one of physical illness. Severe feeding problems have already been mentioned. In some cases, when a child is severely disturbed in behaviour, it may be helpful to admit him to a special hospital unit to investigate the reasons for the problem and to find ways of managing the behaviour. It is most necessary to involve the parents in the investigation and the preparation of a programme of management so that any improvement can be maintained when the child returns home.

VOCATIONAL TRAINING UNITS

Even when an autistic child has been educated in a special school throughout childhood, he will almost always need a further period of preparation before he can find employment. A unit which can provide a gradual transition from school to appropriate vocational training will help to prevent the problems which occur when an immature adolescent has to cope with the adult world. The range of work training should be wide so that each young person can develop his own special skills. The unit should maintain contact with sympathetic employers, and be able to arrange introductions to work in easy stages. The unit should also be closely linked with facilities for sheltered employment.

SHELTERED WORKSHOPS

Many autistic adults are too handicapped to work in open employment, but could be happily placed in a sheltered workshop if one were available. These workshops would probably accept patients with different kinds of mental illness, or mental retardation (and perhaps some with physical handicaps as well). If they are to help autistic adults, at least some members of staff would have to be experienced with their special problems, and a suitable range of work would need to be available.

MEDICAL SERVICES

The problems of finding medical and dental care for a difficult autistic child might be eased if these could be provided at the diagnostic and assessment centres, or at the special hospital units mentioned above. These centres would be familiar with the children's behaviour and could arrange appointments to avoid long waiting times. General hospitals could also arrange special sessions for handicapped children as long as there were staff with a special interest in this work. At least one London teaching hospital has a travelling van which provides dental care at each of the training centres and special units for handicapped children in its local area. This highly successful experiment could with profit be copied elsewhere.

12

The role of parents' societies

Since the last war, 'consumer groups' have started to grow and multiply in Western Europe, particularly England, and in the USA. Among the most successful are the groups representing the parents of handicapped children. The pattern seems to be that the first formed societies represent a wide range of conditions (for example, all mentally handicapped children). Later on, various sectional interests come to the fore, and groups break away to form societies of their own. This seems to happen when the large society begins to achieve some of its aims. Parents of children with unusual problems begin to realise, firstly, that something positive is happening, but secondly that the move forward is not benefiting their own child. Once this feeling becomes sufficiently general in a minority group, it prefers to leave the original body and start on its own.

Some people feel that this pattern of growth is harmful and should be resisted. The argument against this is that the smaller specialist groups have the knowledge necessary to help their children, and that their needs really are swamped by those of the commoner conditions if they remain within a comprehensive society. On the whole the record of the smaller specialist societies has shown that they are successful in setting up the necessary services. As far as autistic children are concerned, since the first parents' society began in Great Britain in 1962, many other societies have been formed in different countries and considerable progress has been made both in spreading information about the children's problems and in providing schools and other special facilities.

Parents' societies fill a great need by alleviating the isolation felt by families with an autistic child. Regular meetings, correspondence groups, and society news-letters all help to keep parents in touch with each other. Informative talks on various special subjects can be arranged. Equally useful is the chance for parents to exchange ideas on how to solve particular problems, and to experience the pleasure of discussing with someone who has been through it all. Parents' groups are also acquiring experience in how to arrange parties and entertainments for their autistic children, to be shared with their normal brothers and sisters as well.

Informing the general public, and people with positions in local and national government, is a valuable function of the parents' groups. Publicity has its dangers since it tends to oversimplify, over-dramatise, and paint too optimistic a picture of what can be done, but it forms a necessary background to community action. Talks, leaflets, posters, booklets and films, plus fund-raising activities such as sales, fêtes and the humble suburban coffee morning, each reach a small audience, but, with persistence, have a cumulative effect. Another aspect of a society's informative function is compiling details of all available services. Parents have difficulty in finding these things out for themselves and social agencies who should help are often woefully ignorant.

The provision of more and better services can be brought about in two ways. Parents can act as a pressure group to put their children's needs before the responsible national and local authorities, in the hope that these authorities will agree to provide the proper facilities. The second method is for parents to raise money and start schools or other units of their own, if this is allowed in the country concerned. In Great Britain a system of 'partnership' between the State and voluntary bodies has grown up. A voluntary society can buy and equip a building to be used, as, for example, a school, and then education authorities can pay fees to the voluntary body on behalf of children whom it wishes to place in the school. This way of working has allowed flexibility and the chance to experiment with methods which perhaps would not be possible in a unit run by a local or national authority.

Most recently formed voluntary societies working on behalf of handicapped children have been started by parents, but are open to interested professional workers. A special quality of drive and determination is found in the groups in which parents have control of the organisation. This is certainly true of societies for autistic children, at least up to the time of writing. Parents on the whole are sharply aware of the needs of their children and, compared with professional workers, are less likely to lose sight of the important concrete issues because of attachment to a theoretical framework. Problems arise when the organisation grows too big to be managed by volunteer workers. Then control may pass into the hands of lay administrators, who lack the motivation of personal experience. This difficulty has been avoided in some groups by the employment, in a professional capacity, of administrators who are also parents of handicapped children. Societies for autistic children are particularly well placed to solve the dilemma in this way because of the tendency of the parents to be of above average intelligence and occupational level.

13

Outlook for the future

LINES OF RESEARCH

Research in this field follows a number of different lines. Those which are being pursued in the search for fundamental causes were mentioned in the earlier section on theories of causes of autism.

Other workers are concerned with defining the precise handicaps of the children and the way these change with increasing maturity. They are devising ways of testing exactly how the children respond to problems presented to them, how they perceive pictures, or patterns of sound, how they organise their movements, how well they understand what they see and hear, and a host of other interesting questions.

The answers found by those investigating handicaps are of great interest to the workers who are trying to test and systematise techniques of special education. Many excellent teachers are not able to explain how they achieve their success, so it is important that the essential ingredients of their methods should be recorded and used in training other teachers.

Finally, still on a practical level, research to evaluate the way in which services are working is being carried out. It cannot be assumed that, just because a school, an assessment centre, a hospital unit, or a social work service is set up that it will automatically work well. Careful observation by research workers skilled in this kind of investigation is necessary to determine whether a service is achieving the aims for which it was started.

The hope for the future is that the causes of early childhood autism will be found, and that this will lead to the development of methods of cure and prevention. As far as can be seen at the moment, it is likely to be a long time before these hopes are realised. In the meantime, the important task is to help the children who are already handicapped to achieve as happy and as full a life as is possible for them. The professional workers in the field will carry out the research. It is up to the parents to see that their own autistic children have the care and education that they need.

PROGRESS MADE BY AUTISTIC CHILDREN

A study has been made of sixty-three adolescents and young adults who had been diagnosed as suffering from autism in early childhood. It was found that 14 per cent did well and were functioning at a generally good level. A further 25 per cent made some useful progress, although they were still markedly abnormal. Most of the rest had become less difficult in behaviour although their handicaps were still marked, but a few, particularly those in institutions, had remained unchanged or had regressed. None of the children in this study had received any specialised education, although some of them had been placed in schools with other kinds of handicapped children. It is therefore possible that the provision of special schools could improve the outcome for many children. The workers carrying out this study noted that improvement in learning and the acquisition of skills often continued into adult life. They pointed out that although to be most successful education should begin early, no age can be said to be 'too late' to begin teaching an autistic child. The study also emphasised the importance of providing suitable facilities for further education and training for employment after leaving school.

AIMS OF EDUCATION

Education (carried out at school and at home) is likely to be most successful if geared to aims that are realistic. Almost all autistic children remain handicapped to a greater or lesser extent throughout life. The aims of education can be summed up under four headings. The first is to help the child become an acceptable member of society so that he can live with his own family or in some other community setting. The second is to teach the child to compensate for his handicaps. He needs to be shown ways of coping with the world which are open to him, and how to develop to the full the skills which he does possess so that he is not frustrated by the things he cannot do. The third follows from the second, and is to educate him so that he can find some kind of employment (whether in open or in sheltered conditions) and a positive role in life as an adult. The last aim, which is by no means the least, is to help increase the child's understanding of the world, to produce some order amid the chaos and thereby to allow him to find some pleasure and enjoyment in life.

These aims are modest, but their achievement allows the child and his family to live a full and useful life, instead of having to struggle on from one crisis to another. Aiming too high (perhaps even assuming that education can make an autistic child normal) may mean intense disappointment and eventual rejection of the child for not having lived up to unrealistic hopes.

The teachers and parents most able to help the children are those who find their rewards in whatever progress is made, whether it is large or small. They believe in the value of every individual, however handicapped. The

occasional remarkable successes they accept as a special
bonus, but find their major interest and satisfaction in the
task of guiding each child forward at the pace which suits
him best.

Book List

Clara CLAIBORNE PARK, *The Siege* (Colin Smythe Ltd, Gerrards Cross, England) 1968. An account, written by a mother, of the problems of living with an autistic child, and the methods she used to help her daughter.

Sybil ELGAR and Lorna WING, *Teaching Autistic Children* (Guide Lines for teachers No. 5. The College of Special Education *and* the National Society for Autistic Children, London) 1969. A brief description of the behaviour of autistic children and the teaching methods used at the Society School for Autistic Children, Ealing, England.

Margaret P. EVERARD (Editor) *An Approach to Teaching Autistic Children* (2nd Edition) (Pergamon, Oxford, to be published 1975). A practical guide to methods of teaching and behaviour management.

Beate HERMELIN, and N. O'CONNOR, *Psychological Experiments with Autistic Children* (Pergamon, Oxford) 1970. An account of research work, some of which has been mentioned in the present book.

J. M. G. ITARD, *The Wild Boy of Aveyron* Translated by G. and M. Humphrey (Appleton-Century-Crofts, New York) 1962. A description (translated from two works originally published in France in 1801 and 1806) of the education of a boy found wandering wild in the woods, who showed much of the behaviour seen in early childhood autism.

L. KANNER, *Childhood Psychosis: Initial Studies and New Insights* (Winston, Washington) 1973. A collection of some of the papers on autistic children written by Leo Kanner, including some excellent clinical descriptions.

Julia S. MOLLOY, *Teaching the Retarded Child to Talk* (University of London Press, London) 1965. This book gives practical instructions for parents and teachers who are concerned with language-handicapped children.

National Society for Autistic Children, *Families at Breaking Point*, NSAC 1970. A report concerning the difficulties faced by parents of very disturbed autistic children.

National Society for Autistic Children. Memorandum to Her Majesty's Government, NASC 1971. The Society's views on the educational, vocational, medical and residential services needed by autistic children, adolescents and adults.

M. RUTTER (Editor). *Infantile Autism; concepts, characteristics and treatment.* (Churchill & Sons, London 1971.) The proceedings of a Study Group, which present much of the most recent experimental, clinical and educational work with autistic children.

Lorna WING (Editor) *Early Childhood Autism* (2nd Edition) (Pergamon Press, to be published 1975). Discussions of the theoretical problems underlying diagnosis, possible causes and methods of management and education.

Lorna WING, *Children Apart* (NAMH, London) 1973. A short booklet describing autistic children and giving some practical advice, especially suitable for the friends and relations of a family with an autistic child.

NOTE

The National Society for Autistic Children,
1A Golders Green Road, London NW11.

This society, the first of its kind to be formed, runs an information service and is in contact with all the other societies for Autistic Children throughout the world. It publishes articles, and a bibliography of relevant literature. References to the research mentioned in this book can be obtained from the above address.

Index